NEVER ALONE

NEVER ALONE

GAYATHRI & RAM

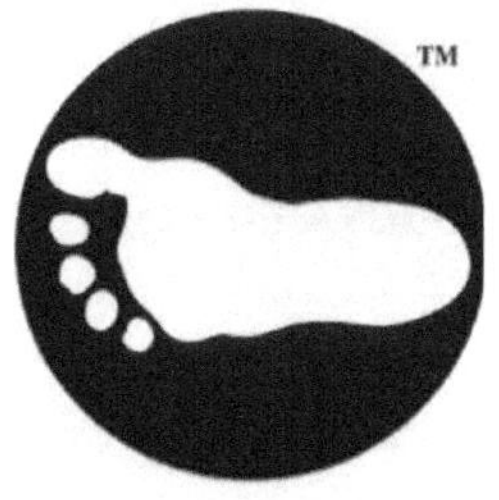

Bigfoot Publications

Because, there's a writer in everyone.

NEVER ALONE

Authors: Ms.Gayathri Ramachandran and Mr.Ramachandran Ganesan

First Published by

Bigfoot06 Publications (OPC) Pvt. Ltd.
211, Muzaffra, Sherpur, Pataudi,
Gurgaon, Haryana (122502)
Website: www.bigfootpublications.in
Email: info@bigfootpublications.com

First Edition: DECEMBER 2021

Copyright © Ms.Gayathri Ramachandran and Mr. Ramachandran Ganesan

ISBN Print Book -978-93-90925-60-5

Although the authors and publisher have made every effort to ensure the accuracy and completeness of information contained in this book, we assume no responsibility for errors, inaccuracies, omissions, or any inconsistencies herein. Any slights on people, places, or organizations are unintentional.

Typeset by PANKAJ ARARIYA for Bigfoot06 Publications

Printed in India

ABOUT THE AUTHORS
Gayathri And Ram

R Gayathri

A post graduate in Finance, and a Ph.D in Education, **Gayathri,** the Correspondent & Principal of **Shri Natesan Vidyasala MHSS**, Mannivakkam, Chennai, India, is passionate about writing.

It was something she started as a hobby, inspired by one of her friends, the **Late Shri. Lalit Modi Ji-** a prominent Chartered Accountant based in Puducherry, well-known for his beautiful and thought-provoking articles that were published in Frozen Thoughts (now called Infinithoughts).

This habit became a bigger part of her life when she joined an online workshop from **Wonder of Words**, a writing program by award-winning author **Megha Bajaj** who has authored several bestsellers, and is also one of the most loved contributors to the Infinithoughts magazine. Through WoW, Gayathri fell in love with the art of writing, leading her to pen her first article titled **"Mathru Devo Bhava"** for Infinithoughts.

And this was just the beginning! From that point, she began writing many more articles, and later became a subject-based content writer for the NCF curriculum books.

When asked how she and her husband started writing together, she says, "While every single article is very close to my heart, the article **"I am He and He is Me!"** is very special. The inspiration behind the article, made us to write together, to bring out the essence of what we felt for each other. Thus began another beautiful journey in our lives, that inspired us to write more articles together."

Ram Ganesan

Ram **Ganesan** is the **CEO** of **SIMARAHITA**- an organization crafted with a vision to deliver outstanding value to the corporate customers, educators and students of academic institutions in India.

Ram, with 28+ years of rich experience working with leading corporate houses, has served in many leadership positions for Fortune 500 MNC IT service companies. Besides his Masters in Computer Applications, his qualifications extend to Leadership Development, Education from IIM Bangalore and Kolkata.

Teaching has been a passion for him starting from the early days of his career so much so that he partook in many corporate training programs that covered everything from technical subjects to soft skills to management topics. He has held critical responsibilities during this period in engaging with Academia throughout the country. These initiatives range from Finishing schools, Campus recruitment and curriculum design. He has visited more than 100 college campuses and schools in India alone.

Having extensively travelled around the Globe and within India, he carries with him rich knowledge of his interactions with a variety of people in the corporate world and outside of it, including students fresh out of colleges and schools. As a mentor, he has engaged with several employees in the areas of personality development, professional skill development, business acumen and soft skill development.

As a seeker, his extensive travel has taken him to some of the most spiritually powerful spaces across the country, which also blessed him with the opportunity to meet with many mystics and like-minded people.

Articles on his corporate journey have been published in several journals. As a seeker, he has always found joy in sharing his experiences through writing as an expression of the divine.

He and his wife Gayathri, both ardent seekers, are passionate about traveling on less travel-worn paths. Together, they love chronicling their experiences through articles.

To our support system - our parents, our angels Abirami and Mathangi, and to several other seekers and like-minded people who have made our journey as writers possible.

We dedicate this book at the feet of the Almighty.

Nothing of us, Everything of HIM.

Introduction:

It all started with our regular reading of "**Infinithoughts**" (erstwhile Frozen thoughts), a wonderful monthly magazine, from the stables of **"Mahatrai Ra".** As regular readers of this magazine, we were inspired by the many true-life stories and life experiences narrated in them. Motivated by a few close friends and well-wishers, we started to pen articles for this magazine, which was accepted by the editorial. We stay humbled for this wonderful gesture. All of our articles were true life experiences, narrated spontaneously in language flow and expression that came to us at that point. We were not trained writers, but as days progressed, we were able to articulate our experiences in a crisp and simple manner. We penned over 75 articles and poetries over the years, all of which got published in the magazine.

A humble vision to publish all these articles in a book form, has at last materialized. We plan to publish all of these **articles and poetries in a series of books,** titled "**Reflections**", each with a specific theme. **The first one in the series is titled "NEVER ALONE",** and others are to follow shortly. We do hope that our articles and poetries, featuring life experiences and lessons of us and about the many beautiful souls we encountered during our journey so far, will be of use to those who get to read it. We have used the words "I" and "We" interchangeably as authors in these articles. This has been deliberately done, so that our personal experiences are not expressed in the third person and the personal touch is maintained.

It would be extremely inappropriate to name just a handful of known individuals who helped us in this journey, as many unknown faces who impacted us by their wonderful conduct of life, have equally contributed to our writings. Words of gratitude will never be a substitute for all those who have partaken in our journey as writers. *Our first daughter **Abirami**, assisting us with the editing work, truly deserves a special mention.*

We consider "Writing" as an expression of the Divine. We lay these books at the feet of the Almighty, seeking his blessings to continue expressing both ourselves and the wonderful people around us.

Pranams

Gayathri and Ram

Foreword

Every once in a meanwhile you meet people, who bypass your mind, and make a space for themselves in the heart. This has been my experience of this wonderful couple – **Gayathri and Ram.**

I met Gayathri years ago, for lunch and we sat under a tree and spoke our hearts out. I knew I had found a friend for life. My interactions with Ram have been fewer – but each time we have met it has been memorable.

Both Gayathri and Ram, stand apart as a couple for various reasons.

First, I love the camaraderie they share – and this book Never Alone, is just the tangible expression of the deep love they have for one another, for travel, for seeking The Higher and inspiring the world. It is the coming together of their life experiences, together, and alone – that have created them, and many along with them.

Second, in this couple, I always sense a wanting to give. No matter what role they are playing, the dominant seems to be one of giving, of wanting to share. No wonder this book is fragrant with love and devotion as it carries their essence of wanting to take you along with them on a journey – outside and within.

Third, I get amazed by how similar and yet different they are. The shy Ram, the chirpy Gayathri. The adventurous Ram, the home and school bound Gayathri. The Ram who doesn't smile that easily, and the Gayathri who will blossom into her dimpled smile as soon as she sees you. I feel this book contains their paradoxes and coming together in a beautiful way.

This book is for all those **seekers** out there who believe, even when they are alone – they are **Never Alone**.

It is for all those **couples** out there who know the Truth of this sentence, "Ever since I found you, I have been **never alone!**"

And for every **adventurous soul**, that wishes to discover itself, in this journey called life.

I wish Gayathri and Ram the very best for their maiden book – Never Alone – and I know they have many, many more stories to share.

For now, let's fill our cups, with these.

Best always,

Megha Bajaj

Bestselling Author/Film Script Writer/ Founder-Wonder of Words

And above all, a fellow, ardent seeker and adventurer.

Preface

Though our lives may seem like they're filled to the brim with everything we could've ever dreamt of, often many of us find ourselves struggling to escape the bubble of loneliness that we've trapped ourselves in. We do not know how it came to be or why it came to be. All that we know is that we sometimes feel hopeless and stifled, desperately looking for a door to run out of.

There are times when we feel like we lack assurance and a support system. We feel so incredibly lonely at the mouth of multiple challenges and scepticism and that terrifies us. But these are also the times during which we actively seek comfort and inspiration- and all these can come from anywhere, out of the blue!

So it is in that vein that we hope that you will find support and perhaps even a solution, as you flip through the pages of this book. Through the articles and poetries, we expect that you will find a friend- a friend who celebrates your joys and successes with the same happiness as you would. Or a mentor that you are looking for to inspire you, guides you forward, a teacher who accepts all your imperfections and says "it's perfectly okay to be imperfect," with a knowing look and an encouraging smile.

This book that you hold, is for the *student and teacher, husband and wife*, the *professional and home maker, entrepreneur and the employees*, for your friend and neighbour and to everyone who would like to celebrate life. This offers something to everyone, regardless of who and what they are - a book that offers a different perspective to each and every person.

This book, in a way is a reflection of every one of our own stories, and a collection of some of our most beautiful memories that have taught us the best things about life.

Come, let us experience the guiding hand of faith together and remind ourselves that we are **NEVER ALONE.**

Table of Contents:

Let's Face it!

Dear God,

You permeate in every cell of mine; still, I feel like talking to you as if you are outside of me… a person, and not just a presence. In the era of social networking, even the husband & wife converse through tools like FB to communicate with each other. So, I thought, why not at least this letter, to you – to me?

As a student I had never been successful in academics or sports or any co-curricular activities, though I hadn't been a failure either. I was just like one of those nameless, faceless students who occupied a chair in school but never a place in the teacher's mind or heart. Never was I able to earn a fellow student's respect or admiration. I should have felt okay about this but I broke down time and again because of the unwelcome solitude I was experiencing. You immediately held me close and said **"Let's face it!"**

That day, when I went up to the stage to give an extempore speech on "Love & God", should I not have been able to speak for hours, as it is about You & Me? But I stammered. I stammered at the sight of audience, which I shouldn't have, as I failed to see YOU in them. I was mocked by few of my class mates for fumbling on stage, during the school function. When I was shedding tears, for forgetting your presence for a moment, my inability to give an extempore speech without inhibitions, you gently stroked my hair and said **"Let's face it!"**

When I took over the assignment of running the family business earlier, with raised eyebrows and a "What does she know?" look, everybody around ridiculed and criticized my induction. Not able to withstand those criticisms, when I was about to give up, you cuddled me and said **"Let's face it!"**

The day, that moment, as I was anxiously awaiting to cradle my two beautiful babies, every word uttered by the doctor, that I had delivered full-term still born twins, jolted me. I was completely shattered by the irrevocable loss. With tears flowing unguarded, as I intensely prayed that what I heard should just be a dream, you wiped my tears, embraced me and said **"Let's face it!"**

Today, years later as I review my life, I am stunned by how far we have come, my God, how far we have come! By myself, nothing would have been possible… but with you here, just giving me the courage to face all the challenges, see where I have arrived. It is your love that has carried me through, my Lord. And see, where we have reached… You and I.

The nameless, faceless student is today the Principal of a school who often counsels students, saying, **"Let's face it"**. The stammering speaker has finally transformed into one who is invited to huge public forums to speak and inspire. The struggling professional is today able to balance her personal life and work life with flair. And the heart-broken mother? She sits today with two little angelic girls wondering how life turned out this way…

It may be ego fulfilling to believe I have done everything – but no, I would be lying to myself. It's all because of you God… but for you I would never have known that this caterpillar could actually become a butterfly.

As this butterfly flutters her wings and hopes to widen her horizon, she just wants to stop and let you know this: "Thank you, thank you, thank you, thank you!"

Ever Yours,

My Creator, My Architect

I was on cloud nine, as I sat there in that cosy hall, waiting for that moment to ascend the dais to receive the "Best Entrepreneur Award"

The hall was crowded, yet, I enjoyed being to myself, spending those precious moment in solitude. I felt softened, as I heard the soft, beautiful song from the movie Titanic, played in the background.

Suddenly, my mind asked me this strange question, "What is love?"

What is love? I don't know what would have been my answer as a kid, but as a teen, love was all about hall mark cards and gifts, and saying 'I love you' at least a million times a day to somebody you loved the most.

As a daughter, for me, being around with my father, sharing the countless stories and incidents that happened in my life with him, would have been the most priceless moment. Having said this, such moment hardly happened in my life. My father, though I knew loved me to his life, yet wasn't very expressive at all. And as a girl for whom, love was all about expressing, life was little disappointing. He was a globetrotter, hence, finding time to be around me, was just next to impossible.

My schooling wasn't in any premier institutions. I wondered why I wasn't admitted to any of those "The Schools" but in a neighbourhood school. Hanging around with some of the "Who is Who" of the city would have been extremely cool. But I was made to go to school in either bus or in cycle to 'one of the schools' and almost all my classmates were from normal families raised without any fanfare.

During one of the New Year, my father gifted me a cassette. As any girl would expect, I too yearned for a Yanni or Backstreet Boys. But it was a cassette containing various Tamil spiritual songs like Thevaram and Thiruvasagam, sung by him. As a spiritually inclined person, though I didn't feel unfair about the gift, yet, in the corner of my mind, I couldn't conceal my disappointment.

While in the college, I was asked by my father to sit along with him in his office during my free time. Whereas many of my friends were spending their time in theatres, malls and parks, there I was in his office, taking notes, typing, preparing presentations and documents. Those were the times where I was spending more time with the typewriter and computer, flipping through the files to prepare documents. Nevertheless, after long hours of work, when I presented the document for approval to my father, snip, snip, went my document and with little more editing here and there. Conclusively, nothing of mine and everything of his and I screamed within, that all my hard work had become futile.

Those were the times I had been brooding and cribbing that life could have been little better for me. As I aged a little, those past moments of cribbing and brooding brought out great revelations within self.

My father was not around me all the time, only to gift me the best life, which many could not even dream off. While many of my friends saw an airplane just in the sky, I had experienced that several times. Whilst most of my friends had just learnt about historical places and famous tourists spots across the Globe, only through their text book, I had experienced it all.

The school led me beyond textbooks by instilling to lead a simple life with high moral values and uncompromising honesty. My experience of moving around with heterogeneous group at school made me a level-headed person in the industry and not a high flyer with attitudes.

What I thought as a boring exercise in my father's office, was truly an experience that only a premier management school or a big corporate could give. The praises from my industrial peers that I receive for my inter-personal, public relation, accounting and financial, troubleshooting skills and for the impeccable documentation work; I owe it all to him. Only that, it took me a while to realize that a father's love is one of the greatest influences on one's personality development.

In personal front, during those turbulent times of losing my twins, I was still sane because of the deep-rooted spiritual life, he had gifted. The only companions during those days of depression were those Tamil spiritual songs from Thevaram and Thiruvasagam, which helped me to be functional, soothed me during the time of distress and subsequently few years later, gifted me two angels too.

The true love is something that everyone wants to feel, but it is a fact that only a little part of the people has the luck to meet her. I felt blessed that I was one of those few lucky ones.

I saw him only as a father while he was trying to be my father and guru. With tears rolling from my eyes, I understood what he has given me. He gave me the best of world, best of knowledge and experience, which for many, is a distant dream. It just took some time for me to realize this.

A father's love for his daughter is a never-ending, undying, unconditional sense that is so indescribable that no dictionary can define it.

Abruptly, I woke up from my past, as I heard my name being called in the dais. Amidst thunderous applause, eyes sparkling in pride, I ascended the dais and held the award very close to my heart. More than the award the words coming from my industry peers were enticing to make me stay further, yet, I opted out only to rush to my car, to drive down home, as nothing gratifies better than the appreciation from my father.

I drove down, to lay the award at the feet of my father.

My Father - My Creator, My Architect.

Infertility Unhurt

"Which is the way to Madam Prathiksha's office?" I asked the girl skipping in the playground. Immediately, with a grin she exclaimed "Oh! Ammaji! Follow me Sir, I would take you there!" She ran towards the gigantic building, which reflected the stature of Prathiksha. As she whizzed through the staircase at ease, I walked briskly to keep up with her speed.

She took me to a young lady clad in T-shirt and Jeans and murmured something to her. The young lady, with a broad smile came towards me and introduced herself as Sanya, working as a volunteer in "Gurukul". She led me to a small semi-furnished room and asked me to wait for the arrival of Prathiksha.

As I sat with eyes closed, resting my head on the chair, I walked down the memory lane. There she was eight years ago, Prathiksha, as a bride, looking so beautiful, adorned in gold and maroon embroidered madi saree. Her husband Venkat mirrored her happiness. Everybody was captivated by their beauty, charm and the unbound love that they shared between them. They prayed and blessed them for everlasting love and happiness.

However, what started off on a happy note, started waning after a couple of years, when the obstetric reports grimed at them with negative results for fertility. Suddenly everybody on Earth presumed themselves as messiah, suggested all form of spiritual and medical advises so that a little one could grace this couple's life.

I had to leave for Boston to take over a project but I had to see my dear friend Prathiksha before I left. She was bubbling with enthusiasm when she saw me, but, the dark circles around her eyes and blemished skin, evidently proved that she was not completely herself. I felt outrageous with God for usurping the happiness of a wonderful couple, in the name of childlessness. Simultaneously, I admired her for facing this fate with her usual cheerful optimism.

After the usual exchange of greetings, "Prathiksha, I want to say something, yet I worry that my words may be unwelcome!" said I, nervously.

"Sriram! When did you learn to ask permission to talk to me?" she asked. She knew what I was getting to, as I could see tears pricking her eyes. But, the soft encouraging smile on her face, revealed how much she valued our friendship and my words.

"Prathiksha! Do you see what you are doing to yourself? Test after test hasn't done anything good for you and it has taken a toll on your health. Though you know the result, you want it to lie to you!" Softening my tone, I added, "Dear, these visits to doctors, astrologers, poojas and yagyas are not taking you anywhere. Don't you see that you are walking in circles expecting to reach somewhere?"

She whimpered softly because of her helplessness to answer me.

"I am bit angry with God because he is upsetting an angel like you! But I re-iterate what you say always. "No Life Exists without any purpose, destined by God". Perhaps, you are destined for greater purpose and not for mundane things in life!" as I spoke, she suddenly interrupted me.

"I think I am getting what you say! You want me to adopt a child, right?" she asked amidst a sob.

"No. That is not what I exactly meant though it is a wonderful option available before you. When two strangers could adopt each other in the name of a beautiful institution called Marriage, then why not adopt one more to complete a family?" I paused and gave her the space to ponder upon our conversation. There was stillness in the room.

After a while, I broke the silence. ***"Please seek what gives you satisfaction and happiness. In the name of childlessness, don't orphan yourself!"*** I pleaded.

Prathiksha, gazed at my face, in silence. After few minutes, she spoke, "Thanks, Sriram! I feel better. I will contemplate over everything you have said!" Then with that characteristic naughty smile of hers she asked, "So, when are you back from US! Don't be gone for too long, okay?"

As I was smiling to myself about the last time we had met, I suddenly felt a presence in the room and was brought back to

"Prathiksha's Gurukul." "Hey Sriram! My goodness! What a surprise!" the voice I knew so well said, happiness dripping from every word. I looked up to see the radiant, beautiful Prathiksha carrying an almost a year-old child in one arm.

As she came to hug me, "Amma, Amma!" a scream pierced the air. A naughty looking boy with two front teeth missing burst into the room and said, "Ananth snatched my ball and refuses to share it with me. He pushed me and hit me and punched my face and the blood came out like fountain from my knee and elbow! It is so paining!" He rushed to hug her and show her all the places where he had been hurt.

Prathiksha said, "Shriram, can you hold this angel for a second, I will be back very quickly", as she said, she left the girl with me and parted in a hurry, to settle the scores. After a while, she came back, both exhausted and exhilarated. The little girl, who was sitting on my lap sucking her thumb till then, at the sight of her mother, began to bob up and down to get Prathiksha's attention.

I opened my mouth to speak, but words seemed so frivolous. Prathiksha took the baby in her arms, gave me an amazed look and said, "I know Sriram, I know! You were my God-sent messenger. Your speech was an eye-opener. After you left for the US, I pondered upon our discussion and after deliberations with Venkat, I realized that **I felt such bliss, such divinity in the presence of children that we decided to adopt not just one but as many kids as possible"**.

"You know what", she continued, "Prathiksha means "awaiting", like my name and I too was awaiting the arrival of a bundle of joy. But it took me a while to realize that "Prathiksha" also means "HOPE". Tears shone through her eyes. I didn't know what to say, so I just looked down and saw that the baby had nestled close to Prathiksha's heart and gone off to sleep with a content look on her face. **The little one knew; she was with her mother and that's all that mattered to her.**

Lost and Found

Ramya was on cloud nine, when the doctors confirmed her pregnancy. The pregnancy made the already pious, soft natured Ramya, much gentler, humbler and devout. She knew this is the time to nurture her "Prahlad." From dawn to dusk it was divinity and divinity alone she experienced. Every little kick, here and there, and every little nudging, here and there, made Ramya blush in happiness and excitement.

That day once the little kick became little in-tolerable, she knew it's time that her baby had become big enough to find its way out! It's the time when both the mother and baby had to work as a team. However, she became little anxious as she felt her team mate was not co-operating. After little struggle, her anxiety became true. She survived the pregnancy.   But she alone survived. A few days later she came back home with heavy heart.

As the news spread, some cried and some were shocked. "Why this, that too to Ramya and Raghav?" wondered many, while some even questioned the existence of God.

Few of them, came to give her that warm hug and the much-needed solace. However, they were surprised to encounter Ramya though little disappointed yet remained a strong woman, full of hope and with confidence that this too would pass and not a wailing, sad or shaken one.

It was indeed a big blow for this wonderful couple. But watching Ramya trying to look normal left Raghav more concerned and worried. "Why isn't she even crying or venting out her emotions!" He felt traumatized.

Unable to bear the gloom, he sat beside her and gently placed her hand on his. "Dear, we will sail this together as we had been so far. Speak out, just speak out, take my shoulders" said he, in a soft, soothing voice and held her close to him. "Why should I? Will that bring back our child?" asked Ramya, as she looked up his face, for answer.

Raghav couldn't answer. At the same time, his worries multi-folded. "Is she out of mind? Is she senile? Oh no, is she getting into depression mode?" thought he.

As if Ramya read Raghav's mind, she said, "I wouldn't say I am alright, but I am trying to recoup from this set back. Just to get that solace, should I curse God? And will I get that solace? HE is the one who gives us everything, holds us close to HIM always. Does HE not know what his children deserve? Does HE not know we shouldn't get hurt?"

"But, Ramya don't you think you are trying to be way too philosophical?" intervened Raghav.

"Do you mean to say that talking about God is philosophy? It's the way of our life, Raghav! It's THE way of our life. Like you, I too am little disappointed because it had been such a wonderful journey for both of us and I bore the kid for ten full months! Is it possible to understand HIS play, for you and me? **Let's trust HIM, as we had been so far. HE knows to take us through this and HE will.** If we are destined, we would cradle our kid, yet again. Till then, why should we worry about "why" and "what" and "how" and "when?"   It is HIS problem and let HIM worry about it. Not us Raghav, not us," said Ramya with a soft smile.

Raghav for the first time discovered a new spiritual, brave and mature Ramya, he had not noticed before. With pride and affection, Raghav hugged Ramya, gently stroked her hair and planted a kiss on her forehead, as a tear fell from her eyes and settled on his palm.

Yes, they have lost but they would find, if they are destined to. Till then, why should they even try to explore or discover HIS designs and plans? **They just wish to go with the flow, holding on to HIM tight.**

The Support System

Adolescence is one of the most memorable parts of life, both for the parents and the kids. Yes, it comes with the package of ups and downs, grim and grins, embraces and embarrassments! Yet, it is the best part for both parents and kids, where strong emotions, feelings and bonding develop among the parents and their kids.

This February, I too as a proud parent, *should have* started to experience the wonderful journey of ups and downs with my twin-boys! *Should have!* Unfortunately, it is in the past tense that I have to write!

It's been 13 long years since I lost my kids, for no fault of mine, for no fault of the doctor, for no fault of the hospital! But, all in a snap, it just happened! Though I tried to unravel the mystery behind the misfortune, at some point in time, I realized that there was absolutely no point in trying to explore the *unknowable!*

I was kept alive, because of the support system called 'my parents'. Whenever I threw tantrum, broke down, felt shattered about the irrevocable loss, they were there for me. Their staunch devotion to God, soothing words and warm hug, helped me calm down. However, whenever I read the mind of my loving husband, hiding all his emotions, trying to put up a brave face in front of me, I felt like ripping myself apart.

I wondered how long I am going to take to comprehend the reality. How long I am going to trouble those good souls? I didn't have answers to fill the vacuum. I stood before HIM. My throat choked; I had no words to express. No words! Tears streamed down my cheeks. But I knew HE is my only strength, my only shield.

The Lord, He is, knows what to give you! HE knows what to do with you! On a fine morning, I had a visitor in my office. The short lady, clad in a simple yet elegant saree, smiled at me, showcasing her pretty wrinkles proudly. It was **Visalakshi Amma,** whom I had met a few years back in a spiritual congregation. A person, with whom my interactions were very limited during my stay, now came with a request whether she could be part of the Education project I was involved in, since she had shifted her residence near to my office!

I was in a look out for a person with similar taste and thus, we stuck the chord instantly. What started off as a professional relationship, became a relationship beyond definition, beyond human understanding. It became the *unknowable*. The day began with strenuous work and ended with beautiful, life transforming, positive thoughts. The more I spent with her, more I felt energized, enthused and encouraged.

So was the interaction that I started developing with one of the unit leader of our organization, **Parimala Gandhi**. Our conversation, slowly, grew beyond our profession. Every conversation with her was breezy, peaceful and relaxing.

These two lovely ladies made me look forward for the 'the best' and not to live in the past. They gave me enormous strength which gradually stimulated me to be positive and to remain positive. Their power of determination and devotion changed my belief towards life. I learnt to smile, to laugh and to believe in miracles, yet again. After a year, my time to sing lullabies happened.

The present life that I, my husband and my parents, relish, feel excited is in the giggles, laughter, pranks, fights and hugs with my two girls - a *'present' by* **HIM.** I wear a smile today and I wish to say, I don't live my past!

Yes, my turbulent past is over! But *'did I'* ride past the tumultuous times of yore? *'Did I'* overcome the restlessness?

A deep sense of gratitude surfaced my mind towards those mystic relationships that I experienced with the God-sent Angels, who made me recognize 'Life is Being Positive'. Who were they? Why did they come into my life from nowhere? How the unknown became known to me? I try not to explore or ruminate.

They were the support system sent by HIM, to rescue me. *There are many such support systems that HE keeps sending to us, when we are down, depressed, shattered or devastated. It is HIS way of reinforcing his presence in our life.*

A warm hug, sharing a simple yet profound message, a chat over a coffee or even a two-minute telephone conversation with one of those Angels, brings about huge transformation. Transcends us, to a greater level. To be blessed with such support system, all we need is to trust HIS ways.

This February I may not experience my boys' adolescence period but in few years from now, I would get ready to be of support to my girls, during their beautiful, unique period of life called adolescence.

As I thought about HIS love, I cried. My throat choked and I had no words to express. No words! My eyes became wet. Tears fell down like 'pearls' as the Ever-loving God made me realize the pearls of wisdom.

Hold on!

I know the fear of Fear haunts you.
The fear of falling.
The fear of forgetting the path you started on.
The fear of fingers pointing at you.
The fear of voices jeering at you, and of your own going unheard.

The fear of being left to grapple with the darkness on your own.
All the times you slipped, all the times you tried.
All the times you fell, all the times you cried.
Wishing for someone at your side,
To offer respite.

But halt and listen, let your frustrations fade and let the tears dry.
Envision the people drifting your boat, the ones you've never
known.
See that they struggle the same way you do,
Take comfort in them standing right by.

Cling on to your raft, it's alright to be scared.
Cling on to your faith, just a little more.
The tough seas haven't turned rough yet,
For He swims below you, pushing you to the shores.

Mathru Devo Bhava!

As I looked up at the clock casually, I was startled to see the time was half past four. For any working women, going home by 4.30 p.m. would be a blessing, but for me, a minute beyond 4'O clock, is like encountering a catastrophe. Cursing my stars, I rushed back home.

Once I reached home, I realized that I may not be blessed to even have a cup of tea at peace. Hence, I slid through the backdoor, made a cup of tea and settled in a chair near the dining area. As I took few sips, I heard a scream piercing the air. For a stranger, it may be something to panic about. But for me, it is something I had got accustomed with.

I pledged not to move until I finished my tea. But destiny had decided otherwise. A little demon in disguise, came rushing towards the kitchen, saw me, and amidst crying started complaining about the other demon with which it was waging a war! The other demon in disguise, sensing the trouble she may get into, came to justify her act. I miserably failed as a referee and in the process of explaining their stand, they were again at loggerheads. As they collided with each other, the little demon tripped and tossed my cup of tea. Glass shattered and my tea, my cup of solace, lay spilled across the floor.

I felt extremely furious. Furious because, as a CEO, I had absolute control over the few hundred employees of my company, and yet with these two daughters of mine, just six and four years of age I felt completely at tenterhooks. They seemed to defy every rule in books on parenting and I just didn't know how to approach them. With my employees, a single rule worked for all – but here, just with these two I constantly found myself wondering what to do?

The role of motherhood had eaten up my personal space. I hardly had time to be myself, enjoying a bit of music, reading books, even eating or sleeping at peace. The job at home had been even more strenuous than my office. So often, I felt gifted because, at least at office, I had little bit of time to relax, but at home, I had to work with clockwork precision to get everything right.

Though hearing sermons about motherhood was enlightening, living up to the demands of kids was a herculean task. In spite of giving up everything in the name of being a "mother", still at the end of the day, there was something found "wanting" from my end.

Tiredness and frustration encompassing, I whacked both of them and left them crying. As I moved out of the room, I was stunned to see my mother staring at me in shock. Though I intended to explain my stance, I failed, as I knew I couldn't justify my act. Blinking back my tears, I ran towards the terrace to spend some time in solitude.

After pacifying my daughters, my mother came to the terrace. As I was getting ready to get shouted at, she gently said the words, "I understand your pain dear! But by whacking them so hard, have you attained peace?" Her soft voice and soothing words brought back the tears in my eyes.

"Mom, what have I not done to these kids? Why can't they understand? From waking them up, giving bath, feeding them, getting them ready to school, helping them with their school work, reading books, singing songs, playing, everything I do Mom! Even if I am late by half hour, the home transforms into a devastated battle field, with papers, books, clothes, toys, everything strewn all over the place. Taking care of their needs, cleaning, organizing…. I am exhausted Mom! All the time they can't expect me to be around them. If I simply vanish, is it going to be their end as well?", as I vented out, I sobbed.

My mother gently stroked my hair, allowed me to cry for a while. At last, when she felt that I am done, she spoke. "Tell me one thing, at office are you a mother or CEO?" she asked.

"CEO, of course!" I answered indignantly!

"Then, why are you trying to be a CEO at home?" asked my mother, "why are you always trying to get everything right?" In an instant, everything about my thought process changed and I was ready to listen.

"Dear, at home your kids don't require a boss to control or dictate terms, but a mother, under whose umbrella they would grow without inhibitions, feel safe and extremely happy." With a knowing look, she added, "The songs they sing, the dance they do, the pranks they play, don't you cherish those growing years of your kids? Don't you beam in pride when you narrate those incidents to me and to your friends?" she paused, turned around to leave and said one last sentence before parting, **"You don't have to prove yourself as a mother – the way you have to**

**prove yourself as a CEO. Here, you just have to be... and
thereby, let them be."**

I stood there with folded arms, in introspection, allowing the
gentle breeze ruffle my hair. Somehow, I felt like my mother had
left the terrace taking a huge weight off my shoulder along with
her. I felt so light. With a smile playing on my lips, I came
downstairs. My two little angels were talking to each other.

The elder one said, "Today my teacher taught me a sloka.
"Mathru Devo Bhava".

"What does that mean?" asked my little one.

"It means that our mother is like God. The way Yashodha Ma
loves Krishna, our mother does too. We worship Yasodha Amma
no? So, it means even our Amma is God! Got it?" asked the first,
feeling proud of her explanation.

"Oh! Now I understand Akka! I saw on TV that Yashodha amma
plays with Krishna, feeds him, makes him sleep and sometimes
even hits him. Just like our amma, right akka?" said the little one,
proud of her understanding. The two giggled, hugged each other
and started playing with their dolls.

With a soft smile on my face, I joined them. Something told me, **after six years of motherhood, I was finally ready to become a mother.**

God in Small Things!

Even before I roll out of the bed, tension would pull me from all directions. Getting the kids up, giving them bath, making them to eat, organising their bags and move them into the car to enable them reach school on time! Huh! The very thought makes the sweat trickle all over my body! But the most terrible part would be to wait beside the car, awaiting the arrival of my driver, to drive my kids to school.

With every passing day, the stories that he unfolded to substantiate his delay in showing up for work, made me feel that he had evolved more as a professional story teller.

Nonetheless, can I afford to sack him? Leaving aside his school time stories, he is a person of integrity, always stays positive, patient and does not become stressed out at other drivers or by their bad road manners.

And I need to add one more, **I don't want to drive!**

Although I '*knew*' to drive, it was always a '*no*' to drive, for me. I never felt driving a pleasure but pressure. Somehow, I had trapped myself in the '*driving phobia*' that it was becoming difficult to break myself out of it.

However, the day to drive, happened too soon than I imagined.

That evening, I clearly gave instruction to my driver that the next day morning the kids cannot afford to start late, as the school was to begin little early than the usual time.

Next day morning, I and my girls, huffed and puffed and got ready to board the car much before our target time. However, in spite of the clear instruction, my driver did not show up for work! The sound of tick-tock of the clock, didn't bring any merry to my mind, instead steam of anger gushed out of me.

What would I do? In another ten minutes the kids should be at school! Though the school is just three kilometres away from home, during peak hours of traffic it would take at least twenty minutes to reach. I scouted for an auto but all in vain. Oh! I was really stuck.

My kids understood the situation. At the same time, I couldn't bear to see the disappointment in their eyes.

That very look shook my core that I couldn't hold on to my anxiety of driving any more. I should get behind the wheel. I was ready to face the fear.

"Come on girls, get into the car!" said I, while I fished out the driving licence from my hand bag. "Hey! Amma is going to drive us to school!" laughed my second daughter. "Uhoo!" screamed my first daughter in happiness.

Though I drove recklessly through the traffic, driving at high speed, dodging the drivers, to reach the school on time, my girls trusted me so much that they enjoyed everything around them. They chucked and giggled, chortled and crackled, as they amused each other.

As I hit the brake to avoid bumping onto a vehicle, they reeled with laughter. Caught in the serious strain of the stress bug, furious I became. "Will you girls, just stop and allow me to drive!" I shouted.

The car engulfed an eerie silence. Suddenly, my first daughter with a naughty smile floating on her lips, mimicked my voice and said, "Girls! Will you stop?" With just those words, she cracked the silence and my sombre mood. That very instant, I too burst into laughter, thinking for sure, my lungs would burst if I didn't stop laughing.

I dropped them at school, just in time and took a U turn to reach home.

As I drove back, tears of happiness peeped out and made me do some serious thinking.

I had given more potency to my responsibility of driving them safe and I left my stress and strain on them. While I focussed more on the frightening experience of driving, they enjoyed the delightful experience of their mother driving them to school.

They were not worried whether their mom would be able to drive them safely. There was no trace of apprehension whether their mom would help them reach school on time. They believed me more than I believed in myself and all that mattered to them was to enjoy the present. Such a simple souls, they never allowed my stress affect their happiness.

I realised, when I have to get them ready every day, then why at all do it with tension? My anger, fret or frustration anyway was not going to bring the driver early to work, then why get upset? When I didn't have any option but to drive, then why should I make a fuss about it and pass on my pressure on others as well? Instead of believing somebody why not believe in me?

I do agree that during the testing times, it may sometimes be hard to feel at ease. At least we can avoid rubbing our tension on others. **Turbulence and happiness are two sides of a coin. Why not try to be on the happiness side? It may be little difficult but it is not impossible.**

When pressure takes over, we lead ourselves to believe that there is no time for laughter.

My girls had taught me beautiful lessons in that moment of laughter. There is no better time than the present to laugh, to laugh as much as possible, as hard as possible, as often as possible. Let us not miss out even a small opportunity to spread a smile, laughter is even better. Apparently, nothing can make one's mind feel more alive, more hopeful and more ready to take on the world than to laugh. **Come on! Let's laugh like my girls, laugh like the kids! Let's experience the God in small things!**

Grand's Day Out

Isn't summer supposed to be fun and relaxing? But how could I call it as joys of summer? While the withering heat and school vacations come together, the kids give you minute-to-minute updates on their boredom levels and above all the tough job of being a referee between them!

'She pinched me - no, she did it first! She kicked me - no, I didn't do it on purpose! I want to watch cartoons - no way, I want to watch Harry Potter! She tore my book – but, she first broke my pencil! She doesn't share X-Box with me – no it's a lie!' The very thought of the tug-of-war and the earsplitting screams of last summer, still gives me goose bumps.

Oh! How I dread this summer! What shall I do? Even before the summer vacations could begin, my summer depression had begun!

Not wanting the history to repeat itself, I initiated my day with prayers to 'Google Devtha!' My hunt for the *engagement-classes* during summer for kids, commenced! Astrology to astronomy, singing to swimming, drawing to dancing, chess to creative writing, crafts to cookery, skating to storytelling, I explored it all!

My mother observing my zombie-like behavior and the *tamasha* happening at home, "You are making such a drama at home!" said she, crossly.

"Amma, don't you know it is impossible to have them at home! And such classes are just to enhance their skills. They learn so much and have fun too!" mumbled I, unable to face her sharp look.

"This kind of *engagement-classes* is just not acceptable. Even sleeping and eating seems to be a luxury for the kids! They deserve a break as you do! If I had managed you as a child, I think I can manage your kids as well! It's been sometime since I and your Appa visited our native village. We would take them to our native village for summer. I am sure there would be lot of learning and fun there too! Leave them to us." as she spoke, I intervened, "But, no one can manage them except me Amma. Unless I am around, it is too difficult to keep them engaged!"

"I wish not to hear any 'Ifs and Buts.' Period." said she and went ahead with her plans, not waiting for my affirmative or otherwise reply.

My usually fussy girls, this time jumped in joy, as they carried their bags and baggage. With laughter and giggles filling the air, holding tight to their grandparents, they bade good bye, as I watched them baffled, wondering what was in store for their grandparents!

There is this complexity about being a mother. When the kids are around, we complain, crib and cry that we don't have enough time for ourselves. When they are not around, we complain, crib and cry that we don't have enough things to do for ourselves!

How could I alone be different? Beyond a week I couldn't sustain without kids!

Ours is a small village with a very pleasant atmosphere. As I reached, I could hardly believe my eyes. A sight that made my jaws drop!

My *'chubby cheeked, dimple chinned, curly haired'* dolls weren't there anymore.

Two small figures, completely drenched, disheveled and dirty, with mud squelched between fingers and toes, playing around with a dozen other small figures, equally messy as theirs, noticed me from a distant, screamed "Amaaaaaaa......!" and rushed towards me.

After exchanging hugs and kisses, they ran away in joy to join their friends.

My girls were full of activities, in a world they had not known till then. They rolled on the rolls of grass and then on the mound of hay, to their heart's content. They were … what they were to be. They ran around the green meadows, helped village women to milk cows and buffaloes, watered plants, tended the calves and what not! There was no one around to instruct them the *'Dos and Don'ts'* yet; they did it all smilingly, happily, cheerfully!

I had impressed upon myself that I am the *'know-all'* of parenting - the only capable person to teach and preach my kids *'the what and what not – how and how not'*. How ignorant I had been?

The grandparents and the grandchildren have this adoration, unconditional love and joy in one another's existence. Grandparents stop ageing in the company of their grandchildren, while the grandchildren turn wise, as they are exposed to the wisdom and wealth of experience of their grandparents.

What I assumed as impossible was made 'possible' because of their absolute love and faith for each other. What is this mysterious mystic connection between the grandparents and the grandchildren? As I thought of the magical bond between grandparents and their grandchildren, my eyes turned moist.

My father didn't fail to notice me. He held my hands and asked, "Gayu, aren't they experiencing the true experience of the life?"

"Yes Appa. No screams, no rules, no gadgets, yet so much of fun and learning! No soft skills training can gift them this experience!" I paused and leaned on his shoulder.

He understood even before I could utter anything. "We too have come through your phase dear! Please don't hurt yourself by feeling guilt. What are we here for!" said he and gently stroked my hair.

The unconditional love, encouragement and support that the grandparents offer to their grandchildren cannot be defined or described by mere words. Grandparents really are "grand."

JUST Me!

Chandrika was both happy and anxious. Happy, because after eight years (that's when her first daughter was born) her husband and she, were planning for a pleasure trip to Europe. Anxious, because she didn't know how she would survive without seeing her kids for twenty long days and nights!

Both her daughters, eight and four, were the apples of her eyes. As a dedicated software professional, she had seen many promotions; accolades and appreciations come her way. However, what really thrilled her was when she experienced her first bundle of joy. First time on that wondrous day of her promotion, she found her eyes welling up, in contentment. Yes, this time her promotion was not yet another professional one, but a promotion as a mother.

She was this epitome of motherhood, who would miss a few hours of good sleep simply to watch her little angels, cooing or laughing. She became sick when she saw her kids sneezing or coughing. She even quietly started avoiding long travels and came back home as soon as she could from work, only to cuddle her darling girls. The doctors had a tough time handling her rather than handling the ailing baby, as she broke down sometimes watching the child getting injections. She would rattle the doctors by shooting questions on the whys and hows!! Oh, she really took being a mother seriously.

Her husband, Tarun, was immensely proud about this doting mother. However, the thought that she had taken her role as mother far too seriously bothered him. He often felt that this single role made her so myopic that for everything besides her kids, her vision was blurred. This left him sometimes feeling suffocated. As days went by, the unrelenting love and affection that she showered upon her kids left him restless and sometimes even mildly irritated. He wondered whether the exuberant Chandrika he had known disappeared? She seemed like a shadow of herself - where was the real Chandrika?

He knew he had to somehow persuade her to look at life little beyond kids and job. There was a life that had to be led for oneself too and he had to make her experience that! Again, once again. His mind, thus, began brewing with thoughts of a holiday… just the two of them. A magical trip…he had a strong feeling such a trip would change things in a wonderful way. Perhaps Chandrika would remember that there was much more to her than being a mother.

Chandrika too was excited and did every bit of planning for this extraordinary trip. However, every inch of her being was occupied by the thoughts and worry about her kids. Would she be able to enjoy this holiday away from them? Tarun too was going to miss his darling kids but he knew sometimes it was okay to be just Tarun, rather than Tarun the daddy.

Tears prickled her eyes as she bade goodbye to her kids. Throughout the journey in the flight, she was worried whether her kids would be wailing or throwing tantrums or falling ill because of her absence, but Tarun kept reassuring that everything would be fantastic as they would be having a rocking time with their adoring grandparents. Even after they landed in Switzerland, the white, icy paradise on Earth, she was too impatient to know how the kids were doing. Tarun remained silent hoping his plan would somehow work. With surmounted thoughts about her kids, she hit the sack, only to bring back those two pairs of twinkling eyes and charming smiles alive in her dreams.

There was no alarm clock or any hustle bustle tight schedule to attend, hence, Tarun left her to sleep, sleep till her body and heart wanted. As the extreme tiredness and jetlag relieved her bit by bit, Chandrika slowly but reluctantly opened her eyes, only to wake up to see through the window, the vibrant, breath-taking view of beautiful meadows against the backdrop of snow-capped Alps. She was happy. She was thrilled. She was ecstatic.

The greens meshed with the whites and blues of the landscape, the cuddle-worthy cold weather, and just the fact that there was nothing to do, but be, made Chandrika feel like a new woman. She jumped out of the bed and exclaimed "Wow! Tarun, this is incredible huh?" in a tone so alive and full that Tarun couldn't help but smile. He hadn't heard this chirpiness in her voice since quite some time. "So, what is the schedule for the day?" she asked, and then paused with a blushing smile, and continued, "If there is a schedule that is …"

Tarun, with his usual soft smile replied, "Snow Sports sounds exciting… but, only if you want to.."

Chandrika was in a state of euphoria when he pronounced "Snow Sports". This was something that she had done when she went on a trip to Kulu-Manali with her sisters a decade ago. Few hours later, Chandrika was in a state of trance as they rolled across Alps. Screaming, shouting, laughing, giggling they went up, they went down and all around.

Tarun was in cloud nine, as he watched Chandrika from a distance, as she put her tongue out and caught a snowflake and closed her eyes with relish. That moment, she was not a corporate executive, wife, daughter or a mother. All that she was, was Chandrika.

Just Chandrika. Nothing else.

The Teacher Was Taught!

"Total chaos in XI B... a bunch of hooligans, I say!" I overheard somebody talking in the corridor near the staff room. How could somebody make such an unpleasant comment about my class? Until now I had believed that my kids are the best behaved in the entire school! I immediately climbed to the second floor of the building, huffing and puffing, only to see that the comment was justified.

With both anger & betrayal engulfed, I couldn't react but could only stare at the class, which had transformed into a cricket ground. All the boys were playing hand cricket and papers were strewn all over the floor. The most disturbing part was that the team was led by Nasir, the class representative. He is such a darling, brilliant boy who always brings an intelligent perspective to the topics taken for discussion in the class. I rubbed my eyes to see whether what I was seeing was indeed the truth? Unfortunately, it was!

"Class", I screamed and the entire class came to a standstill. The boys were trembling in fear and especially Nasir hung his head in shame, unable to bear the ferocious look in my eyes. I couldn't bear to see my star students being so undisciplined and disorderly.

I couldn't control my tears as I knew I had failed in my duty of chiselling them into fine art pieces who maintain the decorum of a class even when a teacher is not present, and hence, with folded arms walked out of class which made them look even sadder. All the boys trailed behind, pleading for forgiveness. I walked into the staff room, scribbled the permission letter for half a day leave stating health problems as reason, handed over it to the security, stationed outside the principal's room and walked out of the corridor.

Nasir stood near the entrance gate with folded hands, with tears streaming down from his eyes. Anybody would have been simply moved by the look on his face. But that day, I was so mad that I didn't. Instead of giving a glance towards the boy, I kicked my Scooty to life and zoomed back home.

While driving back home, as the cool air swept away the sweat, the tears and the anger, I replayed the events happened at school. I asked myself, whether I got hurt because of the unruly behaviour of the students or was it because my colleagues who were waiting for a chance to point their fingers at my otherwise wonderful class, had finally gotten lucky that day? With mounting embarrassment, I realized that after all they are kids and not some specimens in museums. Belatedly I understood that *I was angry not because of the naughty behaviour of my students, but because my self-image got a hit among my colleagues.*

Regretting my act, I reached home and I was startled to see my mother standing beside the main gate. Immediately sensing the seriousness, I took a 'U' turn and drove back to school, only to be greeted by Nasir and the grim Principal near the school main gate. I was deeply embarrassed and walked in the office knowing what I would get that day. The principal would not be happy with such childishness from a teacher.

Nasir began to speak, "Ma'am, I am so sorry about what happened in class. You are not just a teacher but a mother, a friend and a guide to all of us. We just got into the heat of the moment and let go…" The principal smiled at me. My heart was beating faster. I couldn't believe my eyes or ears so I just sat there, still. He continued, "Ma'am, we know we have let you down, but it won't happen again." He pointed to a few more students standing in the corridor, with their heads hung low.

I couldn't help it. The garb of teacher slipped and tears fell from my eyes. It was I who should have asked for forgiveness for my behaviour, it was I who had behaved way out of order and over reacted about a simple thing and yet, here were the boys – barely fourteen and fifteen, readily apologizing, unable to see their teacher unhappy. I went and hugged each one of them and whispered to them, "Please forgive me." The principal nodded in encouragement. They looked embarrassed and relieved and took my hand and walked me to the class. The entire class was sitting in absolute discipline and there was pin drop silence. I just whispered to them and said, "Today each one of you have taught me what love is." **Silence and smiles passed between us. We all knew, that day, we had learnt something invaluable.**

The Teacher and The Taught

Am I a teacher, I wonder?
When I learn to teach, I am.
When my students teach me to learn, am I?

I unravel the mystery of the books for them,
And to me, they unravel what it means to be a teacher!

I am no enlightened being born to dispel the darkness of
ignorance,
I am but a collection of memories of smiles, frowns
of discussions, deliberations and acceptance.

I am not the garb of sternness that most perceive me to be
I am a friend, a mentor, a guide... and a student too!

All that because I step in as the Teacher
and leave as the Taught.

The Teacher and Taught aren't too different,
they can both be the same thing.

Throw away the veil, and you will see
that you can learn a lot more than what you can teach!

Am I worth it?

"Beep! Beep!" sounded Kala's alarm clock at 5.30 am. While she pushed away her bed sheet to get up, she was little startled when she noticed the date of the day – 3rd of July!!!!

The 3rd of July happened to be the most revered "Guru Purnima Day". The day that reminds the teaching and the students' community to celebrate the richness of the Guru-Shishya Parampara that was in existence in our country and also gently reminds the gulf that exists between them and the need to seal the gulf. But, why should Kala get startled about this day?

For Kala, the teaching profession was an accident. A Post Graduate in Finance from a premier institute, she worked as the Finance Manager in a top MNC for almost five years. Later, Kala happily quit her high paying job, to be with her kid. Once the kid turned four, unable to be away from her child, she joined as a teacher in the same school where she had admitted her child.

Initially, Kala had a hard time understanding her roles and responsibilities. A teacher was told to be 'like' a mother, yet, she was not even allowed to scold when the kid did something wrong! As she would enter the class with series of assignments to be solved, the time would vanish in thin air while sorting out the mischief, the fights, the laughs and the smiles that passed between the kids during the class. As a teacher, if she was expected to handle one problem, it looked as good as handling hundred problems at a MNC, as there were too many 'ifs' and 'buts'. But such a strong and determined lady she was that she did not give up on her new role. Slowly but steadily, she began to understand the nuances of handling her new assignment – *Being the Teacher!*

Last week she felt little weird and strange when the school wore a festival look with spiritual fervour, as everyone were abuzz and active in organizing and planning for the Guru Purnima Day. As she wondered what this Guru Purnima was all about, her colleague explained, how Guru Purnima was celebrated by the students to show their reverence and respect to the teachers.

Hearing her colleague explain, Kala thought, "Since there is no Guru-Shishya Parampara, why this celebration? How can a teacher be respected as that of a Guru? Though a teacher is referred as 'mother' yet she can never be 'the mother!' Then why make them look like Gods?"

Are we worth all this reverence? Am I worth all these celebrations? She kept asking herself.

On the D-Day, she felt squeamish as she sat along with her colleagues, watching the children from various classes presenting songs and dance in praise of Gurus and teachers. The culmination was when the higher secondary students offered flowers to their teachers and some of them even prostrated and sought their blessings.

Shocked by these gestures, Kala thought to herself, "No Corporate Company celebrates their employees like this. The employees do their job and they get their promotions, increments and incentives based on their performance. Period. Then why so much fuss about the profession called "Teaching?" We teach. Period. Nothing else. Why such celebrations? Am I worth it? Are we worth it? She kept asking herself again and again!" Yet she couldn't find an answer.

As if to answer her questions, the top corporate guy turned School Chairman, ascended the Dias to offer his felicitations to the teachers and students.

As Kala wondered what this corporate guy turned school Chairman would speak on Guru Purnima, he spoke, "You may wonder what I can speak about teaching and teachers! Honestly the millions of money that I earned are no match to the satisfaction that I gain from running this school. What I am today is all because of the blessings of my wonderful teachers. You may be astonished, why Guru Purnima should be celebrated? But I ask why shouldn't Guru Purnima be celebrated? Yes, there is a gulf between the definition "Guru" and a "Teacher" and they both cannot be kept in the same pedestal. A teacher may not be the *enlightened soul*, yet, is she not the person who while teaching "Gravitational Force", makes the child understand the cycle of life too? As she disciplines the child, is she not teaching him the right attitude? As she scolds him about his poor performance, is she not reminding him to never to give up? Beyond the campus, she may be just another person in his life, but within the campus isn't she everything for the child? How can a teacher who plays the role of a mother, father, friend and a guide be compared with a corporate executive who deals with men, machines and money? Today's teachers may not be the Lord Krishna or Ved Vyas or Dakshinamoorthy who dispelled the darkness and showed the path of wisdom. Yet for the child, the gentle pat, kind and understanding words, makes the teacher *his Ved Vyas* who dispels the ignorance and spreads joy"

After a brief pause, he continued, **"A teacher, who teaches the subjects with dedication, commitment, love and passion can no way be inferior to the age-old Gurus of our country. Should this not be praised? Should this not be celebrated? If we don't celebrate our work, who will? So, take pride. Let's celebrate the teachers!"** said he and went back to his seat, amidst thunderous applause.

Kala who heard the Chairman speak, with awe, closed her eyes and thought, "I may not be that "Enlightened Guru," yet, by following the footsteps of those great gurus, if I could bring about a positive change in my students, is it not worth all the hard work? Making the kids believe in themselves, by giving the gentle pat, words of love and care, will that not transform the child for better? Can money be the yardstick to measure the job satisfaction? NO. This smile, this hug, this celebration from the kids, makes it priceless. **When I strive to earn this celebration, yes, I am worth it"**

Big tears fell from Kala's eyes, as she thanked her Teachers, who had chiselled to turn her into proud and passionate teacher, worthy of the celebration!

You are Worth It!

It was a Sunday morning, the monsoon at its best.

With the monsoon breeze blowing, the sky beautifully cloudy, the Earth smelt like heaven as the rain drizzled around me. "Aha! This is the best time to have a hot masala chai!" thought me, and quickly rushed to the kitchen. In a few minutes, I was in the balcony, holding my hot masala chai cup.

As I took few sips, enjoying the soft and comforting rain, I felt like announcing to the world "This is LIFE!" Suddenly, the urge to pen down my thoughts occurred and, in a jiffy, I was back in the balcony, with my lap top.

As my fingers swung and danced on the keyboard, bringing life to my thoughts, abruptly my inbox popped out with a message for a new mail, which halted my flow.

A simple upward curve decorated my face, as I opened the mail from my niece Rohini.

However, when I started to read the mail, the smile simply vanished.

"Dear Chitthi, I have always looked at you as my friend and not my aunt. Hence, I felt like sharing few things with you, which had been disturbing me for a while. I have scored very good marks in my tenth board exams and you do know that my ambition is to get into IIT or a premier institute equivalent to it. But of late, I am afraid whether all my hard work would go in vain. With mounting pressures from all quarters, I really do not know whether I can do it, whether my choice is right! I dread to even think about a little break!

Reading the mail, I felt little down. Honestly, I couldn't think of a day where I had burnt the mid night oil, to score marks. I studied to score good marks, to carve a niche for myself. At the same time, I had a fair share of fun during my growing years as well. How much the present-day kids miss out on fun, because of the pressure to perform! It is a race they have to run, whether they like it or not. The killer instinct has to take over or they will be killed in due course. How sad! Why can't they study and have fun too!

The rain was incessant. There is this magic about rain. It falls on the trees, gardens, pastures and roof tops. It falls on the window panes and in to your heart, which makes the heart go, merry go round. Rain freshens the environment and refreshes one's soul.

The beauty of the nature around me, made me feel light. I closed my eyes to pray to my lord to help me convince her, that her choice is right and it is ok to live life too.

With prayers on my lips, I just allowed my fingers to go with a flow.

"Darling Ro, most of the kids, after tenth, enter eleventh with dreams of carving a niche for themselves in the profession that they intend to take up in future. To achieve that, they do a lot of homework, like planning, organizing, structuring, scheduling, managing and so on, so that they don't fall behind in the race.

The consistent 24X7 chanting by parents or sometimes even teachers is, "You ought to be a doctor, doctor, engineer, engineer, IIT, IIT" adds further stress to the already distended pressure experienced by that student, who is made to eat, sleep and drink subjects.

Eventually, what started off as a passion for performance, slowly transforms into pressure for performance.

The kid, unable to handle the demands and stress loses his self-confidence, self-esteem, spirits, drive, which many at times, results in descending performance and sometimes bring about some devastating effect as well.

My plea not only to you but all kids like you are that, pressure can motivate for a while, however ultimately it is the passion that will spur you on. This life, you can either get everything right and yet feel unhappy or make a few mistakes but be happy.

Yes, striving for excellence is a must. It is an attitude that must be developed. Yet, excellence should never become a stress. What is the point of that 98% that comes at the cost of health, stress and so much anxiety? Work hard, enjoy working hard, but there is no need to do anything for others approval. Important thing is, you need to approve of yourself. Do you?

As long as the passion for performance is intact, it is OK to lose out a mark or few, once in a while. It is OK to take that coffee break with the Potters and Cullens, sometimes. It is OK to have a rendezvous with Sachins and Sanias, occasionally.

*You deserve to enjoy your adolescence as much as you deserve to do well in studies. A balance must be found. A balance will be found when you begin to enjoy your studies, for the sake of learning and not scoring. Let these amazing years of your life be amazing. After all, **you are worth it**. Love."*

Discipline- Not just a Word

It was a much-awaited trip for us to Taipei, Taiwan. A few dozen school children and senior teachers, most of whom had not made any significant international travel, were really excited to visit our international partner school, Tur Ya Kar ,as part of the educational and cultural exchange program.

A warm and affectionate reception that we received from the school, made all of us feel at home. Be it the classroom, cultural or the game activities, in spite of language barrier, the kids mingled with each other so well. In addition to the several activities that we were part of the fixed agenda, we were taken for a small tour around the school. Every one of us, were awestruck by the infrastructure and technology that was in place at the school.

As we went around the school, one of our students made a significant observation. ***The school had no compound walls around at all!***

We were very eager to ask the Management of the school about this unique feature, during the meeting that was organized subsequent to the school tour. However, we needn't wait till then, since the answer came to us automatically by way of several aspects we observed in the school.

Everything at the school was done as per a defined procedure be it a small activity of the kindergarten students or a board meeting for the executives. To instil a sense of belonging among students, the entire campus was cleaned by the students and even the small kids of Grades 1 and 2 were taught to repair their furniture so that they would take responsibility of their action.

Once the lunch break was over, we couldn't find any teacher around to blow whistle to indicate that it was time to get back to class. Instead in a matter of a minute every kid, right from kindergarten to higher grades, all of them were back to class, ready to learn.

Taiwan, an island known for being hit by sudden typhoons and thunderstorms, there was hardly any trace of any catastrophe that a typhoon had created the previous day of our visit, in the campus. All the stakeholders of the school had got together in bringing the campus to normalcy.

Everything seemed to be so well organized. Nobody asked for instructions and despite that, the event was moving along perfectly. All of us realized that there was a sense of perfection in whatever they did, right from the top management to the kindergarten student.

There was a lot to take-away from the trip. But I felt the most important lesson was the discipline, which was just not a word. It was something that was integrated in their life, knowingly or unknowingly. Hence, there was no need for anyone to enforce anything. Discipline was willingly embraced. It became an inseparable part of their culture.

There were no restrictions and yet, the students knew where to stop. Here, discipline was not defined as a measure to control one's action. It was an inbuilt mechanism to chisel them into better human beings.

Now, I had the perfect answer to my previous question. There was indeed no need to build physical walls around the school. Everyone knew when to leave and when to enter the boundaries.   All of them seemed to live discipline!

52

When discipline is embraced in whatever we do, it is bound to reflect on everything around us.

'I wish I could' to 'I would.'

Pain Or Gain?

My students were all around me to express their joy about their 12th standard exam results.   While they shared their happiness about their achievement, they didn't fail to reveal some of their *so-called* haunting experiences of examinations!

"We owe all our achievements to the teachers, Ma'am. However, I should also mention, the very thought of preparing for exams, was enough to make the strongest of stomachs empty its contents." said Anitha, one of my students.

Another student standing next to her complained, "Gosh! How many sleepless nights! How much we had to prepare for those awkwardly worded questions and we were expected to answer something that was mentioned in one lecture for three seconds!"

"Exams are not a test of knowledge but they are a test of speed", a student in the crowd, divulged her *gyan* and continued to disclose her wisdom. "Don't take it as an offense Ma'am. The teachers too didn't make it easy for us. 'Can you write ten essays in an hour? Now solve a hundred quadratic equations in next ten minutes!' and the list like this goes on. Their hounding didn't end there. They made us look even more worse, when every time they finished their sermon with 'Remember, you have it easy, in our days we did twice as much in half the time and no one ever got bored'" said she, in a voice imitating one of her teachers.

"We ended-up vomiting a string of words that might have something to do with the subject and left the evaluator the joy of deciphering scrawl that even doctors would take pride in!" winked the fourth one.

I watched them all taking a dig at us, with folded arms, smiling to myself about their ignorance.

When their chuckles and giggles settled, "Dearies! I understand preparing and writing exams are not all flowers and loveliness. Aren't you all now in euphoric state, as you exhibit your happiness about getting admitted in Medical, Engineering or Courses of your choice? How did it happen? Was it all a magic?" asked I, with a smile, waiting for an answer.

The girls stood in silence, without an answer.

"My angels, I agree that you all had dreams to make it big in your life. Nevertheless, your notion that even by being a last-minute person you could achieve your dream was not right. This attitude distracted you so much that, when teaching was happening to help you achieve your dream, you were dreaming in the classroom." said I and paused. Some of them chuckled and nodded their head in affirmation.

After a moment, I continued, "When you woke up to the reality, it was a little late. When you were supposed to be revising, you were trying to learn and understand. Apparently, you had to pull up the socks, burn the mid-night oil. Exams are nothing but an opportunity to pull everything you've learned together. It helps you to develop a process, look for patterns, to look for a good way to see what comes up, to focus on revision. There is a comfort in this ritual. If you see studying as a pain, yes, it is a pain! But if you see studying as a gain, it is indeed a gain! **If you are passionate about your dreams, then you should be passionate about working towards your goal as well! You shouldn't be compromising on your enthusiasm and knowledge for the subject.** *Once that realization dawns you, you will happily, joyfully, delightfully, wonderfully transform your dreams into reality. Your achievement today stands as a* *tribute to your hard work,"* saying so, I hugged and congratulated each of them for their excellence in their exams.

Anitha, slowly walked, stood beside me and held my hands. "Ma'am, today yet another lesson was learnt by us in this temple of knowledge and wisdom. ***There is no short cut to success"***, said she, blinking back her tears.

Just Describe...!

With tears welling up the eyes, I rushed to my empty classroom. As I sifted through the pile of letters that my students had written, I wondered why the Principal didn't like any aspect of my teaching at all! Agreed, the kids were excited about the approach for the letter writing exercise, but, if I had to teach only the protocols then would they not be just slumping in their seats, completely bored?

Just then, I heard a knock at the door. It was Jessie, my colleague. "Hey, can I borrow your workbook?" even before she could complete the sentence, looking at my lifeless face, she asked, "Are you OK?"

"I had a rough afternoon. I am just wondering whether I need to continue as a teacher or should I remain a homemaker?"

"Don't even feel that way. I think you are one of the best. In fact, I rate you outstanding" she said enthusiastically, searching for a return smile from my face. "Oh! Thank you for those nice words, Jessie!" I mumbled and handed over the workbook.

As she left, Aarthi, another colleague of mine entered. "You look so lost dear. Is there anything I can do for you?" she asked in a tone of concern.

As if I was just waiting for this question to be asked, I narrated the meeting I had with the Principal, an hour ago, amidst sob.

"Ms. Shetal, there are few points I thought of discussing with you," said the Principal, in her usual stern voice. She leaned back on her chair, leafed through the classroom observation file and pulled out the paper with my name written in bold letters. "I understand from your notes of lesson that you were to teach the concept of letter writing. In the process of teaching, you had told your students to write letters to celebrities of their choice, which resulted in the students screaming and shouting in excitement, and they became little rowdy too!" she paused and looked down at my face, for explanation.

"I thought by adding little excitement they may involve themselves better!" said I, in a low tone.

"But you lost them" she quickly remarked. "The enthusiasm was expressed in number of inappropriate ways. Instead of discussing the protocol of letter writing, they were discussing about the celebrities. Don't you agree?" she asked in an expression exhibiting her excitement about her findings.

"Students, being unstable, require right directions. Stick to the protocol. Perhaps, a discussion with one of the finest teachers, Ms. Janaki, might help. When she teaches, you can hear a pin drop in her class!" she said with every word soaking in pride.

Neither able to defend myself and nor able to express my genuine concern for the growth of the kids, I left the room, by just saying "Sorry!"

"She actually asked you to discuss with Ms. Janaki about class teaching?" Aarthi chuckled.

"Mm… Hmm..." I nodded.

"That's because her students are asleep all the time during her class," Aarthi laughed out loud.

"Aarthi, you joke, when I am depressed?" I burst out.

"Don't get cross; I know how you feel with the constructive criticism by the Principal"

"In fact, Jessie was just in. I wanted to believe her appreciation, yet!" I paused and then said, "When she appreciated about my work all I could remember was those instances where I fumbled and failed"

"That's how it is Shetal! Criticism can knock you off and praises like Outstanding, Exceptional and Great, are too much to take for anyone. People don't realise how to praise, though they mean it. As Frank A. Clark's said, *Criticism, like rain, should be gentle*

enough, to nourish a man's growth, without destroying his roots.
Instead of evaluating, one should just need to describe"

"Describe?" I asked.

Understanding my confusion she continued with her explanation,
"Let's take your own letter writing exercise, as example. Instead
of going by protocols, like address, salutations, subject matter
etc., you motivated the students by giving them the spark of
imagination and thus making them write letters with passion,
purpose and in correct form"

"Exactly!" I exclaimed. "Instead of making it a boring lesson, I
made it interesting and exciting for the kids" As the smile spread
on my face, I said, "You know what, I don't care what others felt
but I am proud of my approach"

"Wow!" said Aarthi, proudly. "See, all I did was to explain and
now you are recognizing the truth in my words and feeling proud
about your work!" saying so, she patted my shoulder and left.

As she left, I pondered about the past events. The Principal's
Constructive Criticism left me hurt and discouraged. Jessie's
overgenerous praise left me feeling unconvinced and unworthy
of the praises. But, Aarthi's *straight forward description* of what
I had achieved restored my faith in myself and gave me the
impetus to perform better next time.

As I pondered, I wondered, *what an amazing process it would be, if each of us could understand the objectives and efforts of one another, share the thoughts and come out with a straight forward, healthy evaluation, so that we could be visible and valued.* That instant, I felt, why shouldn't it start from me?

I smiled to myself and picked up the letters that my students had written that morning, to evaluate.

After evaluating the first paper, as I was about to mark it with a "Very Good" with my red pen, I paused and took out a color sketch and wrote "Dear Tarun, apart from the wonderful usage of words, I felt how much of thinking has gone into your letter, to our Former President. Especially enjoyed your signature statement, ***This is India, a place like none else on this planet.*** I am sure Dr Kalam, would swell in pride to see a youngster like you, presenting a beautiful vision for our country's growth. Good Luck"

My Place of Worship

Every morning that I walk in, I make a choice.
A choice to make a difference
Not just to me, but to the little ones in my care.

With the art I learnt, I try to mould.
I sculpt young minds and lives,
To build a safe environment, I strive.

I guide and nurture, guard and inspire,
To be the hand of God governing His little creations.

Where these hands toil to bring out perfection,
It is no longer a place of work, but a place of worship.

Back to School

April and May are two months of the year when majority of people are on vacation, as most schools and colleges are closed. It is the time for relaxing in exotic locations inside and outside the country or in a quiet retreat at their native place. Parents make all efforts to spend as much as time as possible with their children trying to break away from their busy office or business schedules. These two months pass off in a jiffy and makes one earn for more of these!

Just when all are giving into the slowed down pace of life, June pops up without any wait. The better part of this month is spent on buying uniforms, books, school bags, Tiffin boxes, stationery and what not? Children are all excited with the renewed energy from their vacation and start thinking ahead about their new class, friends, teachers and the difficult subjects too. Come June, it's time for them to be back to school!

While purchasing the **"essential commodities**," as I fondly call them, at a nearby stationery shop, I became unknowingly aware of the many people like me in the shop, who were purchasing 'these' for their children too, to get back to school. Out of curiosity I was looking for a familiar face and I was not let down. I did spot a couple of parents from the school of my children and so also a colleague, a teacher who works with us. After the regular exchange of pleasantries, I asked her the most obvious and rhetoric question! 'Yes, the school for my children reopens in a couple of days and I am here to purchase the **"stocks"** for the year! They are **"Back to School"**, in a couple of days,' replied she, spontaneously. I continued my shopping, after we parted company.

Suddenly, the "Back to School" phrase she referred started me thinking in a tangential thought process. Well, should only the kids go back to school with so much preparation and anticipation? I have been an educator for around 15 years now. It never occurred to me thus far that I also needed to prepare myself as a teacher before the beginning of the academic year. While the meaning of **"preparation"** in my capacity as an educator differs drastically from that of a child/student, the fact remains that this very obvious concept had never taken form in me.

During the lunch recess in the subsequent week, I and a few of my colleagues were casually discussing this subject. That was when I realized that I had company and was not alone! A majority of us were sailing in the same boat. We had never thought of **"us"** going **"Back to School."** Needless to say, this subject now demanded attention and focus more than ever. It could no longer be restricted to a lunch table discussion. We collectively decided to set aside a full day to sit together in a workshop and explore the possibility of making this concept a reality.

The workshop ended up as a great **"Discovery"** exercise, surprising all of us to the extent that we had to break into deep individual introspection for several days that followed.

As an educator, how can I prepare myself well ahead, much before the institution opens up for the next academic year? Have I done enough work to deeply and personally understand my sphere of influence, namely a class or a group of classes or a section of the organization? Each year the student inflow into every class is a variable and the same yardsticks of imparting education of last year may not apply to this new set of students. **I am a fresher as much as the student**. I may be a veteran in imparting lessons in my subject of specialization, but what can I do differently this year which will further increase the impact of my teaching?

Some and many more of these tough but pertinent questions kept pounding us during the workshop, making us wonder as to why are we not **"Back to School"** and why it is so important to be.

The question list kept expanding and demanding too. However, what really stood out amongst all of these important questions was, "Are we as educators doing enough to make the **teaching-learning** process enjoyable?"

Most successful people have become successful only because they loved what they did. When one loves what he or she does, it becomes an integral part of oneself. The commitment therefore to come out with flying colours is not really driven by any external factors or push. The entire process is driven from within and thus passion and commitment are but given components of the process. The outcomes are therefore natural and undoubtedly will be outstanding.

Students today are compelled to look at the outcomes right at the beginning rather than enjoying the entire learning process and leaving the outcome to be an end product of the process. We are a witness to many a student today whom would be able to solve a complex mathematical equation by flawlessly applying a **"standard"** set of techniques. Yes, they would definitely score well in their exams. Not many of them however understand the underlying principles in completeness and therefore limiting their capabilities to look beyond and scale greater heights. While this phenomenon is largely driven by social compulsions today, only those students who enjoy the entire learning process will be successful in their lives, beyond the walls of the school and colleges. Excellent grades are a natural outcome when he or she starts to enjoy learning and is not pressurized by outcomes.

As an educator I promise myself that I hold myself responsible to make this a reality. I will be prepared and willing to go **"Back to School"** as many times as required. An educator is only as good as a learner he or she is. I would like to be the teacher who gives something more than homework!

While I shop for pens, pencils and books for my children next year, I hope to meet the same colleague in the same shop and ask her "Did you go back to school?" I hope to tell her that I did!

Yours Authentically

In today's fast paced world, technology has a significant impact on our lives, day in day out. Starting from the ease of sitting at home and shopping, to consulting a doctor online, the way we conduct our day-to-day activities has changed.

The technology era is a great boon and we are all gifted to be in a knowledge age and in a country, that adopts technology to the maximum. Somewhere down this path, most of us I am sure, would agree that the personal touch is lost and everything has become business like.

Irrespective of the industry segments that we are associated with, this is but the hard truth. Let's take online doctor consultation as an example at hand. As a patient, I now have the liberty to pick up a doctor, specialized in a particular domain, share my symptoms via pull down menus and text boxes on a globally hosted software application. I am even assured of a revert from the doctor in a hours' time. I pay the fee online and in fact even buy the medicines online. The same application even takes me to an online shopping portal that provides me the capability to shop more than just medicines. Oh yes, the software assumes that I am sick and also decides I cannot step out to shop groceries! Creativity and innovation have gone Gen Next.

What a wonderful experience. Have I not saved so much of time and energy sitting in the convenience of my home, hassle free? In the entire process of this particular transaction, I have gained so much and feel extremely elated and feel a sense of accomplishment, a proud user of a particular application. I even rate the application experience at a high five for the entire world to know and benefit from.

But most importantly, more than the sense of satisfaction of completing a hassle-free transaction, I am sure most of us agree that we have lost much more than what we gained in the entire process. At the cost of technology, we have lost one most important aspect of life, the "human touch".

Where is the Midas touch of the family magician whom we used to call the "Family Doctor", who is capable of cure just with his touch, his soothing words of comfort and the bonding that we had created as fellow human beings? Can the invisible doc replace my family doctor, who knew my entire family from my grandparents and could, at the tip of his finger, diagnose an incurable disease without clinical intervention? Did we all not believe in his home remedy for a so called stubborn cold and yet get cured in a matter of hours?

A truth slowly surfaces. We all realize it and a lot of us consciously ignore it. *A subtle but strong factor that goes beyond the visible human relationship stands out. Yes, it is Authenticity!*

Would I ever believe that a cure to a stubborn cold is a small home remedy if it was suggested at a fee in an online portal? On the contrary I would take the small dose of some medicinal juice made by my mother or my erstwhile family doctor, without question or doubt on its capabilities to cure. Why? It's not about the confidence that I have on the medicine, is it not? It's not either about the proximity I have to my mother or my doctor, is it not? It's all about how authentic the entire process naturally played out. My family doctor had only one thing in mind, that I get cured immediately. My mother had only thing in her mind, that I not be pained and get cured the next minute! It was all authentic, right from the heart for me and everyone else. I trust, because I believe that a person is authentic and that there is nothing superficial about it.

The discussions on this continued in the family room after a few days when some of us got together for relaxed evening. Each one had their wonderful experiences to share on the subject. My friend, Ravi was glad to share his association with Muthu and soon after Raj, a corporate personality, chipped in with his.

"For reasons beyond his control, my childhood friend Muthu, took to working as a mason in our small native town. Even today he is just able to make his ends meet," began Ravi.

"Whenever our family visits our native place, the host is invariably Muthu. Our ability to consume three sumptuous full-fledged vegetarian meals, made by his family, every day, can only be limited by the small space reserved in our stomachs for air. Made and served with utmost love and affection we were not only filled with food but with genuine love and affection. The icing on the cake was that his family uses a separate set of utensils, specially reserved for us, for cooking and serving our meals as we are vegetarian when he could probably not even afford two full meals a day for himself. This is a practise year on year for more than 25 years now.   Muthu expected nothing in return. I would hate to canvas this as love, affection or hospitality. Something even beyond these words existed! A meaning, that comes deep down from his hearth, authentic and pure. He is my brand ambassador for authenticity. His influence resonates in my life even today," concluded Ravi.

"A key factor to professional and personal success in today's context is how effectively we engage with our fellow human beings," proclaimed Raj.

I, for example took up **"People engagement"** as a professional focus subject, as the industry I work in, is extremely focused on human talent where people should not be viewed as commodities.

Retaining good talent for the successful conduct of a business is very crucial. I went a step ahead by engaging myself with a mentor and coach who could help me with effective ways to engage with people. For, I did believe from the bottom of my heart that this was indeed one of the most important key result areas that I should focus on. A small step towards being authentic to myself!

My work profile took me beyond our established physical premises to meet with people at far off destinations. Hence the time that I get to spend with my immediate one and two downs got reduced purely driven by necessity. In long sessions, spanning over a year, me and my coach had several engaging discussions on the several techniques that I employ to effectively interact with people. Without doubt they did include how I maximized technology usage during my travel to interact. In spite of my best efforts and his suggestions, I felt several times that I was not engaging enough and the results of my effort were not translating into desired outputs. Something was seriously missing.

The answer came in the 14th sitting I had with my coach. My coach, who was as keen as me, in helping me crack the problem, went on to enquire a little more in detail, as to what I do when I am away from my work place. With whom do I speak, what do I do, how do I spend my time etc. The data that I presented to him revealed a simple but strong message. I had spent a lot of time in inter acting with my customers - people I had come to meet for business reasons and of course my family back home. Nothing unusual that I could see in the pattern, for I had a purpose for which I travelled and felt that I was doing justice to it.

My coach went on and asked, 'What did I do first, each time I travel?'

Well, I call my family, no matter what. I keep them informed about my well-being and keep calling them as often as possible. I also speak and meet with people that I had to meet with almost the same intensity and regularity.

'What about your reportee's and two downs, back home?' asked my coach.

Yes, but not as often. When I had to engage with family I somehow managed to squeeze in some time, means and methods to make it happen, as was the case with my customers. The need and the genuineness were always unquestioned.

' Did you miss your family each time?' my coach asked.

Out popped the spontaneous answer from me, 'Of course!'

'When it came to your reportees, did you miss them?' continued my coach.

A shy defensive "not too much", was all that I could answer.

'When it came to my one and two downs'', I was not seeing it with the same importance as compared to others. The need was always there, but was I genuine for example to provide them with timely updates? By the way, I had people engagement as a top key result area for myself! What it a farce? I pondered.

'Aha! There is your answer beamed my coach with satisfaction of resolving a long-standing problem. My coach rightly pointed out to me that the means and methods I adopt to engage people are good but lacks genuineness. 'You are looking at "People engagement" as a tactical activity and not from the heart. It is not authentic and that is where the problem is, ' concluded my coach.

I felt like I was slapped and it hurt, for it was 'I' who framed my goals. But a hard retrospection at the end of the day, made me understand that I was indeed not genuine. I was trying to engage my people in a superficial way using all the techniques that technology could offer. But what was missing was the real drive at the bottom of my heart to engage my people as authentically as possible. I was looking at this as a **Key Result Area** and nothing beyond it. If I were authentic, I would have missed them as much as my family and customers. Wouldn't I?

Raj concluded his fantastic experience of revelation. As I heard them speak, I learnt a great lesson for life!

From then on, I try not to have any hidden agenda in any of my interactions, be it personal or professional. I try to be honest about my intentions. If I call for a meeting, I make sure that the "True" agenda is disclosed. I have realized that I have become "Vulnerable" by doing this. But I would still be honest, frank and authentic.

As a result, the trust that I have been able to generate over a period of time has made me a better person. I am now able to engage with people much more effectively than ever before. I seemed to have developed a sense of commitment and I feel that people around me have started seeing it and believing it. My work life has started to mirror my private life. It's real, not fake.

But I am sure I am still not Muthu, but I resolve to become like him someday. I believe that day is not too far.

Authenticity is a virtue that cannot be compromised. It takes tremendous courage to be, to tell someone that I am indeed, "Authentically Yours"! Do I have that courage? Oh Lord, please bestow me with that courage.

Picture Perfect – The art of perfection

While driving, it is my habit to hear some good music, a discourse or a lecture to keep myself surrounded by positive energy.

During one such long drive, I heard **Mahatria** speaking about **"Dhinacharya"**, a concept that originates from the Ayurveda. "Things done imperfectly over a period of time consistently, is far superior and yields results better than trying to do everything perfectly the first time!"

Essentially one has to identify the "Weak Spot" in one's professional career or personal life and work on it daily. For example, if I am not good at understanding numbers, but my job profile needs me to analyze financial statements. Rather than shy away from the challenge, if I focus on it and try to decipher it again and again, I would one day become an expert. I would have perfected the art of not only understanding the statements but may even be able to provide expert analytical views on it.

In my opinion and limited experience of the world, there are only a very few people in the world called Prodigies! Identification of a particular talent or trait at a very young age and practicing it over and over makes one very close to a Prodigy. The rest are all Perfectionists!

A visit to **my aunt Ranganayaki Rajagopalan** along with my kids every Vijayadashami day is a "no miss". She is an octogenarian, an award winning veena instrumentalist and a perfectionist of course. Though several ailments had crippled her active lifestyle, yet the very mention of music would ignite her, even at this old age. She never fails to surprise us by playing a few of the toughest ragas on her veena with passion in those ignited moments.

Astonished by her exuberance and energy, my first daughter asked, 'Atthai Patti (Grandma), were you a child prodigy?'

Atthai laughed aloud showcasing her beautiful wrinkles and said, 'On hearing my first kutcheri (performance) at the age of seven, the famous Tamil magazine Kalki mentioned that I was a child prodigy. But honestly, I feel it was because of the training that I received from my Guru right from the age of three and the everyday sadhana (practice) that I did, I am what I am.' After a pause, she fondly hugged her and said, **'If you practice something every day, you too would become perfect. Even to create magic, the magicians have to practice. Practice is required even to perfect magic!'**

I remembered to have read that the legendary nightingale of music MS Amma, used to practice a song for many hours, to get the raga, swara and diction perfect, before each performance, irrespective of how many times she had sung the song on stage earlier. The master blaster's commitment to practice is a well know secret for all the cricket fans around the world.

Let's think a bit deep. Are these great legends prodigies or perfectionists?

Bhutan has always fascinated me in many ways. I consider this place as my personal spiritual aboard. Never do I miss a chance to quote Bhutan where ever possible, in my articles. The GNP (Gross National Happiness Index) country provided yet another opportunity for us to spend time there on happiness break! We had to trek one of the highest peaks, housing a Buddhist monastery and being weak at heart we decided to take a horse ride to the cliff.

The only words that the horse understands were its name and a "click" sound from the owner. While we were so scared to even climb the hill on foot, the horses were at ease. Every step that they made in the extremely rough and steep terrain was picture perfect. They stopped at the right places to take a deep breath, the right places for a water break and also took the most comfortable path uphill considering the rider on its back. We were astonished by the horse's eloquence and grace.

Well, you might say horses are born to do that! The only interesting part is 'We were not accompanied by the owner.' The terrain was new to us and we absolutely had no idea where we were going! But the horse took us to the top, exactly to the place where we were supposed to reach.

On enquiry we found out that the horses climb the 10km slope two or three times a day during peak season and they have perfected the art. We were lucky to be on the back of a Mr Perfect, while some of the others were riding on the "juniors".

Growing up, we have all heard the expression 'practice makes perfect' from our first teacher, our parents and grandparents. **Malcolm Gladwell**, an expert on the subject went on to popularize his research that expertise essentially developed over "10,000 hours" of deliberate practice. But how does that really work?

When we learn a new skill, whether it's handling customers, learning new programming, planning project development, playing chess, or experimenting a new cuisine, we are changing how our brain is wired on a deep level. Science has shown us that the brain is incredibly plastic – meaning it does not "harden" at age 25 and stays solid for the rest of our lives. While certain things, especially language, are more easily learned by children than adults, we have plenty of evidence to show that even older adults can see real transformations in their neurocircuit. Well, in order to perform any kind of task, we have to activate various portions of our brain.

For example, to make a good presentation or a speech, our brains coordinate a complex set of actions involving our motor function, visual and audio processing, verbal language skills and more. The first time around, the presentation might feel stiff and awkward. We might forget some of our points or flub an important phrase. But as we practice, it gets smoother and feels more natural and comfortable. What our practice is actually doing is helping the brain optimize for this set of coordinated activities, through a process called myelination. Myelin, the white stuff in the brain is instrumental in making us perfect! It's the "White Cells" and not the generally referred "Grey Cells" that make you look smart and intelligent. What practice makes is, it increases the Neural Activity and this causes the growth of Myelin, which makes you the perfect Human Being!

I really don't know what those words meant for my daughter when we met Athai a few months back, but it set me up for serious introspection. There is no one stopping me from becoming a legend and it is so quite easy. Is this not what **Mahatria** has been saying, **"Dinacharya"**, all along?!

I guess it's time to go ahead and grow our Myelin and become the legends we always have earned to be. With the dawn of New Year, **I have made up my mind to grow those magic cells called Myelin and practice Dinacharya – at least on one item in my wish list. What else could be a better New Year resolution?**

It's Business As Usual!

The month of December 2015 saw Mother Nature in full fury at Chennai. The rains and floods created havoc, washing away lives and property, on its way into the sea. Social media was abuzz with activity with each one contributing in their own way. Heated debates by social activists, environmentalists, the media and the general public on global warming, infrastructure planning and waterways management gave all of us enough information to digest and make conclusions on what went right and what went wrong.

While we are not going to debate about that, we certainly need to look beyond the noise. A truth that got revealed during those days of crisis once again proved that Humanness was the winner.

There is an old Tamil saying **"Manudam Vendrathu"** which literally means that **everything about humanity won**. Incidents of loot or arson that are generally common during such catastrophes were not at all heard. I don't recollect even hearing a murmur on this, even on the busiest news channels, beaming live feeds of the flood hit city. Instead, we saw, people on the streets braving the rains, risking their own lives going out to save those people stuck in the floods. People went a step more, in taking care of the needs of the brave soldiers and policemen too, who tirelessly were working on the ground to help the common man. Thanks to some great innovation and creativity of many people, technology lent a helping hand in connecting to the world.

Relief material poured in from all quarters, corporates, business houses and the rich. Not to mention, the huge help from the ordinary citizen and the poor, who could not even afford a full meal for themselves. Did anyone ask them to do so? Certainly not. It manifested from within. The value and purpose of being a human being stood tall. It did not know caste, creed or religion as much as the flood did not distinguish between the rich and the poor! All that was seen around was pure compassion and sense of responsibility towards a fellow human being. The business schools are sure to write this down in history as a vibrant case study of a great nation and the culture that has been imbibed in us from times unknown.

As a professional I learnt a huge lesson from the disaster. I was able to redefine **Business Continuity Planning (BCP) and Disaster Recover (DR)** with a very different perspective, which till then was etched in me as another technical subject in Management and Governance! BCP and DR are often the most used "abused" words in corporates around the world. Every organization defines water tight process and procedures to continue with business in the event of an untoward incident or a disaster occurs, generally referred to as **Business As Usual (BAU).** Mock execution of drills every year theoretically prove that BAU is possible after a very short recovery period even to the tune of a few hours. With most business being global in nature one cannot deny that this is a theoretical exercise either.

But wait! Man, machine and process seem to come down to their knees during actual disaster, like what happened at Chennai. One of well know business establishments at Chennai went onto to proudly proclaim that it was the first time in the century old existence they had shut down operations for a few days! One has to look beyond such a statement and introspect about what 'I' could have done to not be in such a situation.

While many of the business establishments were not able to recover to their own self-proclaimed standards of disaster recovery, there were those few that stood out and ran the business in almost a BAU mode within hours! Though personally I had been extremely lucky to not have gone through any difficulty during the deluge, the same was not the case with many of my co-workers. My workplace was located in the area which was one of the most ravaged territory and most of my co-workers hailed from that area.

Getting to know the horrible experience that many of my co-staff had gone through, I could hardly sleep or eat. I wondered how they would ever get back to normal life, leave alone getting back to work! Well, I stood corrected, as a group of my team who were stranded, braved the floods and were at the doors of the organization to plan recovery! They did not carry the "tag" of an employee but became part of the institution that had taken care of them from day one.

When I made it to the workplace after a great deal of difficulty, tears flowed uncontrollably. This was not only because of witnessing the mishap that had happened to my workplace, which had given everything to me, but also because of seeing most of my colleagues, who had come braving all odds. In spite of their sorrows, difficulties and trauma, they came together to make the place - a workplace again. The sorrows vanished and it was all smiles and cheer just like their large hearts! A "War

Room" kind of set up discussed, debated and executed action to perfection. By the end of the day, we had already transformed it to the "Work Place" that we had known, the place that all of us worked together! Back to "Business as Usual!" While this was my personal experience, such was the case with many other business houses too.

What makes recovery so quickly possible? One cannot deny the effectiveness of documented procures and protocols, but I felt that there was something more to it. Yes, there were challenges in power supply being cut off, mobile and data networks not working etc.   But in spite of several handicaps, what unambiguously stood out was the "purpose" of the individuals themselves! Their unstated commitment to ensure that because of "me" someone else should not suffer stood out! The organizations that had built this culture were the ones that stood out. Humanness can never ever be defined in a rule book.

On the contrary a global e-Biz organization that used to boast of the highest levels of customer service and focus were not able to deliver their services even after one week after the floods. I strongly believe that, as an "invisible" organization it could not really create the much-needed Human culture and value systems amongst its partners and employees.

That's where my organization stood out! I hold no shame in boasting to be part of it and more so of a culture that glorifies and worships "Humanity".

The inclement weather proved - **"The Humanity" was the winner!**   As I said, **'Come What May – It's Business As Usual!'**

As the clock struck twelve

Time shrank with decisive rapidity,
Seasons nonchalantly took turns,
Nature's active exposition once again,
Stamped its indelible mark
On the sands of time!
As the World anxiously awaited
The clock to strike twelve!

December nearing its finale

Just around the corner

Willingly waiting to unfurl yet again

Another year of anticipation

Full of promise and optimism

Millions around the globe

Waiting in elated disposition

For the clock to strike twelve!

It's that time of the year!

You and me indulge in resolutions

Assortment of resolves

Varying from the mundane to exotic

An endless list of dos and don'ts

A wish list swelling year on year

Yet nothing stopping from making another

In the year to be born

Before the clock struck twelve!

An idealistic set of promises

Some of which never materialized

For reasons known and unknown

A few accomplished with determination

Others hanging dangerously loose

Will the bucket list ever shrink?

Or will it exponentially grow!

Much muddle and predicament

Before the clock struck twelve!

A seemingly complex predicament

Unremittingly repeating year on year

Brooding over unmaterialized promises

Fashioned from instinctive mood elations

An affair of twists and turns

With no solution in sight

Many around the globe

Waiting to usher another new year

Before the clock strikes twelve!

The silence of the night

Broken by loud fireworks

Shouts of joy and ecstasy

Ringing through the crisp night breeze

Welcoming the new born

Expression of emotions a plenty

Millions around the globe

Waiting to usher the new one

Before the clock strikes twelve!

Sounded a voice from within

Laced with authority and precision

But ever guiding in grace

A perfect riposte

To the complex predicament

Light at the end of the tunnel

A quiet message from within

Excitement! A solution at last!

Just as the clock struck twelve!

Let me live life ever day

Taking baby steps one at a time

The seemingly complex equation

So very simple broken down

No more yearly resolutions

And annual review affairs

Determined effort and commitment

To self-made promises

One day at a time

A complex affair made so simple!

As the clock struck twelve!

Every day a year born new

Every moment so very precious

Gracefully living in the instantaneous

Resolutions achieved in the moment

Engraved within for eternity

Is there a need for new year resolutions?

With a purposeful life each moment

New year resolutions faced imminent defeat

Fading away into oblivion

Defeated by this new-found revelation

As the clock struck twelve!

A life with new year resolves

Was but a thing of the past!

A bucket list tranquil in existence

Teeming to the brim

Yet, this blissful path to a resolute living

Atomically studded with "Every day" New Years

Resolutions and accomplishments are for real!

No longer waiting in anticipation

For the clock to strike twelve!

The Ripple Effect

The much acclaimed **'Pygmalion Effect'** is generally understood as, "When great expectations are placed on people, the better they perform." This has been proved by several scientific experiments over the ages and is quite true too, though some may argue that these experiments are conducted in unnatural circumstances.

The myth of a Greek sculptor, who fell in love with the statue he chiseled, is not something that can be washed off either. So much was his thoughts and actions, focused on creating the girl of his dream that the statue he fell in love with every strike of the chisel, came to life at the end.

My own understanding around this subject is a little different. One thing is about self-belief and the other most important thing is about, how contagious both positive and negative energies can be. The energy that emanated from the sculptor was so great that it bought the statue to life. That is what I would call as **'The Real Pygmalion Effect.'** While the positive is extremely difficult to create and sustain, the negative is an epidemic that can spread as fast as the forest fire.

The other day, my very close friend and a senior executive with decades of experience in the field stepped into the offices of a software company. The company prided of niche products and service offerings. He was looking for a change in job, as the current one was becoming mundane. While the social media and the company websites had so much to say about the firm, the moment he stepped into the premises, he felt that 'something' was gravely missing. The fact that the interview went extremely well and he was even offered much more than what he expected both in terms of salary and designation, he did not take it. The well-lit reception, the disciplined security procedures or the sprawling campus were indeed impressive. But he could feel that "something" was missing. He did find that "something" when he got back home.

Well! What did my dear corporate friend realize that made him reject a wonderful job offer? He realized that a positive energy space was lacking in the atmosphere. This was later corroborated by facts shared by a few employees within, that the company did not have any specific values in the conduct of business, resulting in a space that was void of values. This could probably only be experienced and my friend could have been gifted by the ability to realize it, just by being present there.

Recently, I and my family had been on a visit to the ancient and very sacred temple of *Tamil Saint Manicavasagar*, near Pudukkottai in Tamil Nadu. The moment we entered the temple we experienced something very different. The whole space seemed to have been filled with "something" that was undefinable but one that could be only experienced. As normal human beings, the moment we enter a place of worship our minds race to seek the Divine's help in solving our problems - health, wealth or otherwise.

As we gathered outside the temple, after it closed down that afternoon, all of us realized that we had not asked HIM of anything. We were all engulfed in "something." Period. The great saint that he was, an incarnation at that, and a temple built by him for HIM, was only filled with the positive energy that he had generated thousands of years ago, at that place. All he sang, in his Tamil spiritual scripture 'Thiruvasagam' was all about surrender, surrender and surrender to the Supreme. No wonder we surrendered in that energy and there was really nothing to ask for.

Wait a minute! Did I not feel the same thing when I was at the Tiger's Nest in Bhutan a few months back? The same feeling of being engulfed in something positive and powerful!

Being a somewhat traditional family, often we used to have the recital of one of the most recited scripture in the modern ages, 'Srimad Bagavatham,' at home. The reciter, a simple but earnest and 'authentic' old man, whom we fondly call as *'Bagavathar,'* who became acquainted with us in a long train journey several years back, keeps saying that the repeated chanting of the name of the Lord is what will cleanse the world in the Kali Yuga.

While I really did not understand the meaning for quite some time and its significance, I realized the true impact that it could create, only when I went to the temple at Pudukottai. Each time Bagavathar spent a week with us, our living room used to be engulfed in 'something' that cannot be expressed in mere words. The happiness and the peace that was generated used to last for long, making us yearn for more. The Idiot Box sitting right in the middle of the living room with its baggage of soap operas and news channels, used to wipe it all with ease and grace! So much so that we decided not to sit in front of the TV anymore, except for those small time-pass moments.

Not all of us today may be able to create that big an energy space, as the great Saint Manicavasagar! But we could do one thing for sure. Be positive, feel positive and emanate positive energy.

Wouldn't a very nice good morning, from the bottom of my heart to my co-worker, make him feel good and wanted and in turn, would he not wish the same to another person? I would always want to get off the bed on the "right side" every morning. Must I not wish the same for the next person on the bed? Is this not what our tradition tells us? *"Sarve Janaa Sukino Bhanvanthu."*

It's a chain effect you see and we could create small energy space filled with positivity, by a very small, sometimes even an insignificant act, in the eyes of the others.

Positivity is also contagious and it can become an epidemic too.

Slicing Ego

Getting my Ego down on its knees has by and far been the largest challenge I have faced so far, in pursuit of a better "Me". I might just say that I have achieved very little success so far, as time and again it pops out with the same power of a shaken soda bottle! Over time I have also realized why it has been so difficult to crack this nut. One main reason that I could attribute in conquering this demon, is that it is something created by "Me". Hence, I keep trying not to let go, because it has become so absorbed in me. A creator always finds it difficult to let go of his own creation is it not?

After a tired day, when sleep takes over, I naturally give into it and get into a deep slumber. I really do not try to fight against it and the progression is natural and smooth. A moment of retrospection will reveal that since there was absolutely no resistance from my end, I slipped into a deep slumber. I tried to use this analogy and inferred that whenever and wherever there is resistance, my close friend "Mr Ego" spontaneously gives me best company! Where there is "giving in", he finds my company not worthwhile.

Having understood that this was my own creation, the next steps that I took was to see what were those key ingredients that helped me in creating this fellow. For, if I tried to eliminate those one by one, I firmly believed that I can be a better person, if not a person with ego fully eliminated. I made up my mind to pluck the first low handing fruit and crack it. I engaged systematically in a ***"Five-Why"*** type of analysis, the brain child of the Japanese, who used this method in their pursuit for high quality standards and perfection. Break down larger problems into smaller ones, question and find the root cause.

Voila! It worked. I got to grip with a small component, that if conquered could probably put my dear friend Mr Ego's head down a little bit, if not bring him down on his knees. A self-promotion tactic, nowadays referred to as **"Humble bragging"**, is what my analytics lead me to. This is a critical ego booster. I always want to hear how good I am in the eyes of others and seek appreciation by making self-depreciating statements with the **ONLY** intention of seeking attention and pride.

This is a very common phenomenon that we see day in day out, both from within ourselves and from others and yet we fail to realize that this is a major contributor to fostering ego. I have been in my field of work for more than 20 years now. Though it might sound as self-bragging, I believe that I do know a little bit on the nuances of this field, while I may not be the best. A reputed media house the other day wanted to take some inputs for their research work and hence interviewed me. The first sentence I started was "What do I know about this? I am not such a big person to be interviewed". Honestly deep down in my heart I was expecting the interviewer to say "How can you say this? You are heading such a large organization; you of course know everything about this field!" Lo and behold! It happened the very next moment. The interviewer echoed the question and in turn my humble bragging feathers started to flutter.

My friend took over from then on. My friend Mr Ego had a sumptuous meal to consume, and out he popped out with pride! Many of us will relate to such incidents in our own lives. A very famous personality tweeted "I am number 15 on the runway to take off. How I miss my personal flight!" This humble bragging is about a famous personality flying a common man's carrier! One of my close friends an extremely talented IT professional was just not making it beyond the final round of interviews at many places, in spite of the fact that the earlier rounds were always extremely positive and impactful. A close confidant tried to help him overcome this professional barrier. The confidant came to the conclusion that my friend's humble bragging attitude was what had let him down in the final rounds. For example, when asked what his biggest weakness was, he used to answer that as he was a perfectionist, he could not work with teams. A classic example of humble bragging is it not?

Research shows that 77% of participants in a survey conducted by a reputed organization, had chosen to humble brag rather than disclose an obvious weakness—the most common answers focused on perfectionism (32.8%), working too hard (24.6%), and niceness to a fault (14.8%). Most organization while hiring relatively senior people evaluate organizational fitment as a key parameter and humble bragging is a major deterrent. Science tells us that ego is something very unique to human beings. So, we are actually gifted "ego" by design in that sense! Having said that, should we not strive to overcome this mechanical nature if we wish to grow!

Humble bragging not only adds fuel to our ego, but also puts us in poor light in situations like those described above. It has been scientifically proved that pure bragging and pure complaining is far better off. Of course, it creates negative impression but at least brings us down to reality much more quickly than the falsehood of humble bragging. While normally we have a tendency not to say something negative about ourselves as it makes us "vulnerable," I would consider it a better ingredient in our system than duplicity, as it takes us a bit closer in cleansing us of our ego.

The Almighty has also shown us the means and methods to overcome it.

Whenever a discussion about an ideal person crops up, the first name that we utter is 'Rama'. A name that is associated with high-minded actions, ideal qualities and sacred thoughts. A name that is associated with ethical code. 'Rama' demonstrated by His words, thoughts and actions how such a life can be lived. The name "Rama" is repeated by millions every day because of the attributes and actions associated with the name which has been etched forever.

Humble bragging brings the "Me" component, always to the focus and not my actions or deeds. People are most often remembered by their deeds and not by the figurative form of the individual per se. Certain characteristics are associated with the name and hence the name is remembered and never the other way around. I have realized it is important to focus on the deeds and eliminating the "I, Me" component to the extent possible.

I would have achieved much if I stopped Humble bragging in all forms, entirely. It's indeed a difficult journey, but if I am able to breakdown the ego components one by one, starting with this one, why not give it a try? I am sure working on these small slicing exercises like this, I might find my ego coming more under control without too much of overt work.

I Can !!!

"No, I can't handle this anymore!! I just can't!" I sobbed to myself in the bathroom.

Last year, this time, third time in a row, my appraisals showed "EA -Exceeding All expectations". And that means, a bigger pay packet, greater recognition and above all, feeling like I am a few notches above my colleagues in the corporate ladder.

However, the icing on the cake was when it struck me, those three years of hard work; three years of sleepless nights and a decade of loyalty had paid off in such a big way. I was handpicked for the Best Employee Award, from ten thousand employees of my company.

There I was, on the stage, cynosure of all eyes, brimming with joy, as I received the award, amidst a thunderous standing ovation. I was in cloud nine, when I held my trophy, citation and cash award, so close to my heart, grinning ear to ear. I had a whale of time with extensions of celebrations with family, friends and family and friends. Praises! Praises! Praises! It was raining praises and I heard nothing but "IT" for the next few days.

The celebrations were short lived and I had to come back ground zero, to continue my job with letters, documents, emails, conferences, smiles, likes, dislikes and frustrations. I thanked God, because in spite of all this, he never made me encounter one of the significant emotions - *The FEAR of not performing at work.* As if the Lord had heard my whisper, too soon, I was made to taste the fear of losing. Yes, the fear of losing out from the position of being the 'blue eyed employee', the one with the 'golden touch.'

Earlier, when I heard "Push! You are much more than what you are!" I felt elated. But now having heard this just too often, I knew I couldn't take it anymore. I felt so stressed out. The frequent sickness and mental stress, made me realize that I am not made of nuts and bolts but flesh and skin. I felt like screaming, venting out my anger, steaming out my pressure! But how??? I was, after all, the best employee of the year. And, everyone made sure, I never forgot this!

"You need to be even more vigorous in your approach; you need to go that extra mile, because you are the Best in the organization!"

"I am surprised that you want to leave by 9.00 p.m. You are not a WHO but the Who's Who of the Organization"

"Push Yourself Little Further! You are a born winner! Yes, you can do it!!"

"If not You, then WHO?"

Such words of wisdom and motivation (!) started gaining momentum at a break neck speed and the pressure started reflecting in my performance. The Best Employee got the appraisal rating "EM – Exceeds Most of the expectations", first in the last few years!

More than the rating, the mourning around me, made me feel sick and lost.

The "Is that you" and "Can't be from you" looks pierced me like a sharp knife and butchered me into pieces. The "Fear Factor" started eating up my peaceful life.

Here I was sobbing… unable to handle the fear of losing my status, promotion and recognition.

The eyes reddened and looked sunk in; I splashed water on my face to get rid-off the irritation from my eyes along with the anxiety dwelling in my mind. When I looked up, I clasped my hands and gasped for air, as I noticed my pale skin and the dark circles around the eyes in the mirror. Suddenly it struck me that I had allowed success to get into my head.

For years, I had been performing for the joy of performing, to fulfil my passion and enthusiasm. Somewhere in this process, when the passion transformed into pressure, so much so that today I was wondering if I should even continue in this profession? I had succumbed to the compulsion and competition. I had let the praises, criticism, appreciations and accusations, occupy every little inch of my body.

I smiled, after what seemed like years. I realized what I had to do: I had to work for myself and not to prove a point to someone else. I had to work for the joy of working, and not for the accolades. I had to take a break once in a meanwhile so that I wouldn't have a complete breakdown. As these insights unfolded, I felt so relaxed, almost like a feather peacefully floating in the cool breeze, untouched by any pressure.

Passion for performance, YES!!! Performance on pressure, NO!!! I had learnt, finally, how to deal with success.

Thank God It's Friday!

A phrase too familiar for the white collars, is it not? Who amongst us have not been waiting for that Friday to end and take us into a land of bliss, week on week for years? Every one of us wants to break away from the shackles of the office lobbies, cubicles, meeting and boardrooms. Alas it's something that most of us are not able to achieve as often as we wish to. We pride ourselves in saying that I am extremely busy and don't find time to spend with family and proudly attribute it to the tag of professional constraints or commitments! Some of us may be physically away from work sometimes, but mentally engaged in the so called "professional" set up. On one such weekend, a rare escape from the "set-up", I was gazing at the photo albums of two decades of ours.

Flipping through one of them, I came across the memorable photos captured during my stay in Atlanta, USA. I was amongst the fortunate few, if I could say, to have witnessed the 1996 Olympics at Atlanta in person. The magnificent city that it is today, was almost created for the Olympics. Every other business used to close down by 3.00 PM and for three months it was like our "Mariamman" festival there. It was during this period I took a liking to the wonderful game, basketball and started to follow it so closely, that I hardly used to miss a single match.

As a budding young professional, it was here that I was greatly impacted by a "true professional", **the great Michael Jordan.** He used to lead the Chicago Bulls franchise of NBA then. As was the case, every match he played would take you to the edge of the seat. As I recollect, Jordan would probably play maybe 30 to 45 minutes of a 90-minute full time game. The best part was his last three minutes, which also mostly, was the last three minutes of the game. He would change the entire balance in his team's favour. With critical assists, direct shoots, slam dunks and extreme agility, he would put his team always on top and win the game, for them and him. He was a true finisher, committed to sign off the purpose of his job without a gap. Picture perfect!

The last few photos of the album were that of myself posing in the financial street of the World, Wall Street, NewYork. Rajat came to my mind. Indeed yes, it is the same **Rajat Gupta, the IIT Delhi topper, Harvard Business School alumni, elite CEO of Mckinsey** and then the disgraced partner in Goldman Sachs.

He broke through the racial glass ceilings in the corporate world in a way that no other Indian and few people of colour had done before. So much so, he was much sought after to the likes of the Presidents and influential Millionaires. His climb to fame ended with shame and was recently convicted for 'Inside Trading,' serving time in the federal prisons of the US.

These two contrasting personalities that emerged from the nostalgic moments of the album, led me to deliberate on a debatable question, *'Is the former a true professional versus the latter?'* for each excelled in his own way. Not able to conclude on my thoughts, I closed the albums and my eyes for some time. During those moments of silence, I pondered upon what real *'Professionalism'* means. Both Rajat and Jordan possessed fantastic characteristics of a professional but 'something small' but yet as large as the world, distinguished them. While Jordan is etched in history with the positives, Rajat is etched more with the negatives. I concluded that it is a thin line, "The Lakshman-Rekha ", that distinguishes us between being a true professional versus a "not so" true professional.

Professionalism is not a text book definition that one abides by and gets certified! It is what we live and breathe, in our professional work. The first few hits on a Google search for the word 'professionalism' will show you terms like white collar, executive, non-manual, paid job, so on and so forth. But from the historical meaning from several civilizations of the world, this word originates from **"having professed one's vows"**.

A doctor for example, is a professional only if he 'professes his vows' to cure and save lives. An entrepreneur can truly call himself so, only if he 'professes his vows' to do business with high ethics, integrity and values. A teacher becomes a real-life hero when he/she 'professes the vows' of changing someone's life for the betterment. Indeed, there are certain key elements beyond academic qualification or capabilities that define true professionalism. Would my qualification of a BE/MCA/MBA make me an engineer, software professional, an entrepreneur or a banker? **A true professional goes beyond these boundaries.** These are academic qualifications, but not necessarily the professional eligibility to perform the job at hand. Going a step further, I consider **my domestic help,** definitely not a white collar, a true professional not by qualifications but more so by the **perfection at household work.**

While we may not be privy to personal lives of a Jordan or Rajat, and not necessary as well, I am convinced that there is very little that segregates one's personal and professional life. We might have observed that the true professionals would have been the exceptional Moms and Dads too. Given this context, is there a need to even distinguish between professional and personal lives at the abstract level? How good a person I am will truly reflect on what good a person I would be in my profession!

If I were a true professional, I would also know how to balance life while paying 100% attention to my job and not fail in duties outside of it. I would know how to prioritize with ease, as much as I would be able to clearly demark the good versus the bad. I would certainly be a good professional if I practised highest values and ethics in my life, day in and day out.

In today's busy world aren't we all hiding behind the 'professional tag' and use it as an excuse not to focus on things outside our professional life? Is it truly professional to mark weekdays as 'Professionally work days and weekends as 'Family days'? You will see that the weekday-weekend timelines are mere mental barriers if we practise true professionalism.

The yearning for a Friday dies down and we would all be saying "Thank you God for this day" and not "Thank God it's Friday".

I Would Climb

The bustling building, the foreign voices.
The alien environment, and their unfamiliar faces.
All this and all that overloads my senses,
As a growing determination blazes in me!
I am no duck in the water, but I shall learn,
And I shall climb the ladders.
I may stumble, and I may trip,
But never will I loosen my grip.

I shall ask, I shall teach!
I shall train, I shall coach.
Keep my goals in sight, itching to reach.
I shall push till no boundaries remain,
Reminding myself of where I want to be,
Time and again.

Forward, I will race,
Even when opportunities slip by like grains of sand.
I shall persevere,
Passion always lending me a hand.

Forward, I will run.
Slicing my ego apart.
Work till Mondays and Fridays hold the same place in my
heart.

Forward, I will progress,
With new responsibilities, and zero regrets.

Power Dressing

My younger daughter is passionate about dressing. I don't have the faintest recollection of teaching her the art of dressing anytime! Instead of being her mother's daughter, I guess she must have picked up some genetic stuff by becoming her grandmother's granddaughter or should have been inspired by someone!

Never have I seen her making fuss about the type of food she eats every day, nor the sleep timings or the extra homework from school. However, she is very particular of what dress she wears every day to the extent that we get into arguments almost every day. While I am still not able to conclude on how she picked up such a keen interest in dressing, I did observe one thing consistently. Whenever she wore what she liked, the energy and enthusiasm in her stood out distinctly.

Children through their innocence teach the elderly much more than what we teach them. By nature, though she is a soft spoken and a little shy kid, when she was dressed in her best, I noticed that she was overflowing with enthusiasm and was far less constrained, as against her normal self.

Watching my daughter's exuberance, I wondered how I had failed to realize what good dressing could have done to me all these years, in reference to bringing out the best in me. I could now draw a parallel to several times that I had been in my best either at a seminar, a family gathering or a business meeting, was when I was dressed in my best. I am not in any way suggesting that good dressing was the only reason for being at my best, but definitely one of the key contributors.

To further objectively corroborate this finding, what better way to experiment than at the work place where I had influence over a sizable number of people?   Without divulging the purpose behind the exercise, I suggested my team to adopt a resolution that we will be in full formals on all Mondays and full casuals on Fridays and decided to implement a dress code policy.   This is a common practise today everywhere in the world and there is really nothing new about it, except that we embarked to measure the outcome of this exercise.   We went about defining some parameters to measure work efficiency and productivity over a defined time frame.   Aha! The results were almost in line with my hunch.

The efficiency and productivity on Mondays were far superior as compared to Fridays.   I strongly believe that the formal dressing on Monday subtly but surely impacted the way we work on Mondays.   We felt formal and business like and dealt with issues and problems far more efficiently than on Fridays where the casual dressing set an informal atmosphere and along came with it loose and not so structured ways of conducting business. While this small exercise may or may not hold water depending on the contextual aspects such as what should be termed as formal or informal, it does prove to some extent that the way we dress has an impact on the way we deliver and conduct business.

The other day we were attending the wedding of one of my first cousins. This was a traditional wedding spanning three days. As is the case with most such gatherings, all the invitees were dressed in their best dresses, colourful and all cheerful. Nothing like getting complimented on one's outfit so much so that nothing can ruin the good mood for the rest of the day! When we look good, we get noticed as much as the one who is dressed inappropriately. One of the guests was so inappropriately dressed for the occasion that invariably every other person noticed it. I even did hear low murmurs going around to the extent of passing negative remarks on the individual.

Maybe that form of dressing would have been fantastic in another setting, but not for this one. That is indeed why most religions and cultures have dress codes for places of worship, for dressing directly contributes to the purpose.

Appropriate dressing is a form of non-verbal communication. When we look good, people notice. Feeling good about oneself is an excellent reason to dress well. The opposite is true too, if you don't look all that great, people will attribute all kinds of negative traits to you.

Recently, I had to reach to a not so known place in the suburbs of Chennai to meet someone. With the Metro construction happening everywhere I decided not to drive and rather take a bus to the destination. I did not know which stop to get off and was constantly looking through the window for signs of my destination. An elderly woman coming back from selling her vegetables noticed this and gave me instructions to get off at the next stop. Incidentally an office going lady who overheard us, asked me to get off two stops later. I got off the bus as advised by the well-dressed office going lady and realized later that the old lady had given me the correct direction but I had chosen to obey the office goers advise. While the outcome was different, I wondered why I did so.   I did realize that I had made a conclusion based on the not so good dressing that the old lady wore as against the well-dressed woman.   I may have been judgemental in this situation, but I could not overlook the fact that how you dress yourself changes who you are. It changes the value of what you have to say!

Dressing is a form of expression and why would I have to express something negative more so, by in-appropriate dressing. I feel investing around 15 minutes a day to get dressed well, is worth it. Treating every day like a special occasion and breaking out with my best and appropriate outfit every day has contributed leaps and bounds to my ever-increasing confidence levels.

As I invest time in the outer me in the form of dressing, my inner me is benefitting as much. I feel **"I am worth it"**.

Yet another Way ...!

Chennai got to experience the fury of nature when Vardha ravaged the city a few months back. Everything in Chennai came to a standstill. Power supply, the lifeline of existence, was disrupted for a very long time which bought life to a crawl in the city. After the storm, Chennai looked like a war zone with trees uprooted everywhere. No one dared to venture out with gusty winds blowing at 140 Kmph.

I assume that most households stayed indoors as much as we did. Schools were closed; there was no power supply, no TV and very little stock of food. We therefore had no option but to gather ourselves in the living room for hours together.

I reckon with only such situations every person in the family get-together in one room. We at home felt it was a boon in disguise. Minutes became hours, as we felt time was literally crawling at its own pace. The natural choice for "time pass" was to indulge in small talk on a wide range of subjects. Time led us into a hot topic that was doing the rounds at the national level during that time. A heated national topic can't escape even a saint seated in a cave far off in the Himalayas. That being the case, how could we have been insulated from it? The hour-long small talk slowly evolved into a heated debate. Each one of us had very strong opinions about the subject. But somewhere we started to lose the context and the debate turned emotional with each of us taking sides rather than debating the subject. A very familiar situation that most of us would have encountered in our families when small talk actually leads to debate and then gradually raises itself into a confrontation! All that we ended with at the end of precious hours was nothing but sore feelings.

This insignificant incident like many others vanished after some time, just like the tall trees that Vardha had laid itself on, until recently when we were in a workshop discussing about Global Citizenship. We were giving ear to a deep subject called **"Personal Identity"**. The presenter was immaculately explaining where this stems from. With several examples he bought out the fact that Identity lies deep rooted in the community, colour, nationality, profession or even position that we recognize ourselves with. In the context of that gathering and subject being discussed, he explained that with the easing of this identity, the better people we become, while not compromising on our core. I could now distinctly realise why the living room incident that I explained earlier ended up with a sour taste in the mouth.

Our day to day lives drives us to assume different identities. Once we get very closely identified with something, there is all possibility of emotional aspects creeping in. We therefore, most times end up with a rigid stance, unwilling to loosen up our identity. I realized that in the living room that I had become rigid because of the fact that I had identified myself with a personality related to the subject, rather than the context or the topic under discussion. The views I therefore expressed were more of my like or dislike of that particular personality and truly not that of the subject. I was tending to take a stand identifying myself with that personality. I became immune to what others were expressing, though in reality they may have also been identifying themselves strongly with something. The bottom line is a strong identity leads to becoming rigid and hence the possibilities to look dispassionately at things disappear. It is **"My way or the Highway"**.

An example at hand is the prime-time news beaming across our households every day. Everybody seems to identify himself with something and the focus on the subject being discussed gets vastly diluted.   It only ends up with negativity filled living rooms and nothing more.

As an educator, I am duty bound to teach the young generation on what is good and what is bad. While all of us generally agree to what is good and what is bad for the younger generation, I now critically think that I really cannot identify myself as a good person to teach good or bad just because of the fact that I believe certain things are good. I may end up stereotyping my children on the basis of my identity with the good. I have therefore learnt that I can only tell what I believe is good or bad and cannot really force my identity on someone else. For, if I do that, I would in all possibility identify myself as Morally Superior and start to look at others as Inferior. This is especially relevant and for the most part true in situations where we identify ourselves as educators.

I am reminded of a famous quote that goes to say. **"If someone tells me that the sky is green, I simply say okay. I don't need to agree with them and I don't need to prove them wrong or show them proof that I am right if/when I believe otherwise. I simply go on with my life, with a newfound understanding that to some the sky looks green. And I am okay with that, it keeps external conflict from disturbing my inner peace and isn't that where peace begins?"**

One baby step to be at peace with myself, or in others words, identity shakeup would be to avoid conflicts from external sources to the extent possible.   I could, for example avoid discussing a topic that is irrelevant for my well-being during my evening at home with family even if prompted to dispassionately give and take inputs. It may not be humanly possible to avoid all confrontations in our day to day lives but I could make conscious effort to avoid them where possible. Making this one but significant effort to consciously avoid or dispassionately engage, I believe, will majorly contribute in building a flexible identity. I am persuaded to further believe that this will deepen during the course of time and result in avoiding conflicts within me too.

The simplest and the fundamental aspect that I need to do therefore, is to understand that there possibly is:

"Another way and that my way or the highway, is not the ONLY way"

The Art Chain

One beautiful evening, as Tina logged into her social networking page, she was stunned to see a notification from one of her friends who had tagged her in a post 'Art Chain.' She had nominated Tina to post her creations for five consecutive days.

When Tina went through the posts posted by others, she was amazed and startled. She was amazed because of their immense talent and efforts in exhibiting their exquisite work. Some of them had revealed their baking and cooking skills, some of them their paintings and various other art works, the names of many of those she hardly knew and some of them had showcased their specialization in fashionable clothes and accessories. She was startled because she didn't fit into any of the art forms displayed by her friends.

Relatively the easiest thing should have been the culinary skills as it is said that women folks are quite natural like a duck takes to water. But then, having known Tina's exceptional (!!!) cooking skills, everyone around her would agree to disagree. Actually, one of her FB posts which drew the highest number of comments was for the photo of the *semia upma* which she had made! She shuddered of the thought, about the *upma* post, which brought out satire comments from her friends. The billion-dollar question that went viral was 'How Tina's *upma* divorced the *kadai*?'

She knew for sure; she is going to become a subject of mockery. What a mess she had landed herself into because of the social networking menace!

What art form could she exhibit? What skill could she bring to the fore? She is not an artist to exhibit paintings or any art work, nor was she a designer to post clothing or jewelry designs. And culinary skills!!! With just tea and curd rice making skills, what would she post?

"Why am I not good at anything?" she moaned.

While she was contemplating on gracefully quitting FB, suddenly a thought evoked her mind. She may not be a great cook, an artist or a designer and she may not be able to do any of those wonderful creations exhibited by her friends. She definitely would not fit into that segment. But why not post few articles?

As a matter of fact, she is not a professional writer either. Nonetheless, the articles that she pens as a hobby, those which aided her to move towards her creator, helped her count on her blessings, why not post them? Why shouldn't she strive to bring out articles about some of the beautiful souls who by every passing day, through their positive flow of thoughts, motivation and encouragement, alleviate her into a better person?

As this deliberation happened within, a beautiful revelation surfaced her mind. Just because someone is not good at one thing, it doesn't mean that she cannot be good at anything. Just because someone is a better cook or an artist, doesn't mean that she is better than all in everything.

Each of the nature's creation has its own uniqueness. No two zebras or giraffe have the similar pattern of stripes or spots. Everyone is unique in some way and if everyone possessed the same qualities, won't this whole world be a boring place to live? Instead of comparing oneself with somebody about the qualities that we do not possess, would it not be great to discover what we can be good at and strive to become the best at it.

Tina is now not worried whether she would be successful as a better cook than her or an artist than him. She is concerned about what she could achieve through her posts comparing her to what she is capable of.

As Tina read the words of love and tears of happiness that she received from her friends in response to her post, she knew she was good at something.

Drop it!

As I was getting ready to get back home from office after a day of strenuous work, I received a call from one of my so-called family friends (!), who with her sweet coated words enquired about my blissful life! I replied to her in a monotonous voice as I simply couldn't summon up excitement. In fact, hearing her voice was enough to get back all those memories of pain and humiliation that I had undergone because of her. Her jealousy had cost me so much - and here, she was trying to talk like we were the best of friends.

As I banged the phone down after her unsuccessful attempt at small talk, I slipped into the past. Maya, wanted to be chosen as the next CEO of the company but the responsibility fell to my lot. Instead of gracefully accepting it, she rounded up a few of the employees and went on an anti-campaign against me. Fortunately, nothing worked. Unfortunately, she really got me worked up. With a bitter taste in my mouth, I could still remember the humiliation I went through for two entire years until she left the company.

A sea of negative emotions engulfed me, as I looked at those painful events. To bring down the heat, I gulped water from the jug in a hurry. It was then that my phone rang again. Without even looking at the name flashing on the screen, I picked the call and barked, "What do you want?" The caller replied, "Hey, cool it!"

It was the voice which I would recognize even in my deep slumber. The voice, that appeases me, during the times of pain and that shares my happiness, during the times of pleasure. Feeling flustered about my tone I said, "Ganesh, I am sorry! I didn't know it was you!" He chuckled and with his usual witticism, said, "I should have installed a phone with video option. Never dreamt of such a treatment from my darling wife!" His tone then shifted towards concern as he asked, "What disturbs you?"

 "Maya called", I said petulantly.

With a sigh, he asked, "So?"

That was enough for me to get enraged, again. "Don't you know how much of humiliation I had to face? Two entire years of hell! What she did to me, wasn't it a slur on my image? Do I need to narrate how much I had to sweat it out to make everyone realize my calibre and commitment to the organization?" I spelt each and every word, in an ear-splitting tone.

He interrupted and said, "You are talking the past, Sridevi. Drop it. It's over now."

"It's not over yet, Ganesh!" I screamed. "It's not over yet! And now, you don't start your "Drop it" preaching, Ganesh. The past can hurt! Just as I heave a sigh about the ordeal that I got over with, she calls to know how I am doing and how she misses me!" I paused to take a deep breath and calm myself.

Then I continued, "What does she want to know? Do I still hate her or have I forgiven her? Does she actually think she has a hold over my thoughts and emotions even after all these years?" As I spitted fire, I could feel my heart palpitating.

Ganesh said softly, "She doesn't have a hold over you, dear. But you are still holding on to her, aren't you, Sri?"

Instantly, my belligerence dropped. So true, it wasn't Maya who had a hold over me; it was me who was holding onto Maya! In fact, I had been holding onto her for so many years! So often I had mulled over those two years. So often I had drowned myself in a sea of self-pity and wondered, "Why did she do, what she did?" Today, for the first time I realized – what answers was I waiting for? What answers would appease me? Truly, in two words, it was time for me to just "Drop it!"

By saying so little, Ganesh made me think so much. The realization dawned upon me that in spite of me disowning Maya physically; the inner mind had dwelt upon her behaviour, over and over again, making her a part of my life even though she was no longer a part of it. I had continued to carry her into my office each day – long after she had left it. And what had I got out of it? Nothing! Ganesh seemed to realize the feelings I was going through and chose to hang up with a quiet, "Love you."

"How much space does Maya deserve within me?" I asked myself and I could hear my inner voice instantly, plainly, replying, "Not even an inch!" Suddenly I had the image that I was standing at the height of a mountain, with my hands holding a large black box of negative thoughts and feelings about Maya, held too long. I could see the burden, the tiredness, the anxiety on my face in my mind's eye. The whisper, "Drop it!" resounded within and I did. Years of anger, years of self-pity, years of anxiety – dropped.

As traces of "accumulated Maya" from my thoughts and feelings dispersed and dissolved, I could feel myself immersing in a pool of love and peace. I felt cleansed. I felt purified. Such freedom!

I could feel a smile in every cell of my body. I never knew I could feel so light. I closed my eyes and immediately sent a prayer, "Thank you Ganesh, thank you." Holding onto gratitude and happiness was so much better… in fact everything about my life could change if I could internally program myself to say, **"Drop it" whenever there were negative thoughts or emotions and shift towards happier ones. Drop it. Yes, finally, I have.**

The Green Magic

"I am your saviour and you are nothing without me. Without me you are just a grass - weak!" fumed Madhavan. With tears rolling down from her eyes, Malini, extremely exhausted, wondered what she would do now.

She was a simple girl from a small village, living a happy life with her farmer father. Her dream was to become an engineer, but she ended up doing literature, as her father couldn't afford the engineering fees. She always wore a pretty smile, because he knew whatever she did, she would excel.

Even before she could contemplate a post-graduation, her father got her married, as he couldn't refuse a proposal. She wore that pretty smile, because she knew she would handle her new role with grace.

It didn't take her too long to realize that she had married a chauvinist, and yet, she didn't brood, crib or point fingers. Instead, she quit her high paying job as a language translator and became a dotting wife, daughter-in-law and little later a mother too. Though there was never a time called "her time", yet, she never felt that she had sacrificed anything but always felt that she was living in the moment. She strongly believed that one day she would experience a beautiful breeze. She wore that pretty smile and kept waiting.

But today, when her husband wanted to call it quits, she found herself at crossroads. It should have been the other way round – had she borne eight years of humiliation, harassment for nothing? Her husband, with whom she had shared her life for eight long years, today wanted to dump her like a heap of waste. Her in-laws, whom she had always considered as her own, now had turned their back. What would she do now?

Unable to handle this, she called her father and then boarded a train to her village to be with him, to find some peace.

Ramamoorthy, Malini's father, felt extremely guilty and depressed with his decision of dumping his only child into this bottomless pit, in the name of marriage. He kept wondering how his little angel grinned and borne it all, and never complained or blamed him or no one else for her wretched life.

Having understood all the pain his child had undergone; he was determined to stand by her as she was attempting to overcome her bitter past. This, he thought, would also be his salvation for his gravest mistake. Unable to bear the gloom, he took Malini and his grandson, Raghav, for a walk in the fields.

Malini sat in a corner of the open field that beautiful morning, staring at the calves grazing on the luscious green grass. Cute little Raghav, was so excitedly running around the fields, plucking the gras and chasing the cattle. Watching her son pluck the grass saddened her even more. "Why is that I mean nothing at all to my husband, even after all my hard work, compromise and adjustments? Why all my prayers have gone in vain dad, why? Am I just a weak blade of grass, like one of those, dad?" Malini broke her silence and asked amidst sobbing.

Ramamoorthy, sat next to Malini and lent his shoulder to cry on, to cry her heart out.

Once he knew, she was ready to listen, Ramamoorthy spoke, "Dear, I don't know why things didn't work out in spite of all your sacrifices. But I am certain that this is just the beginning of a wonderful life ahead of you. And I assure you that I would be a pillar of support. Just let go dear, let go, the bitter past. It's going to be a fresh new lease of life for you!"

After a pause, wiping her tears, he said, "Malini, **do you believe the grass is weak? Don't you know that this simple, slim,** green plant is a survivor? It can survive grazing, trampling, burning or drought as long as it is not uprooted. It holds to the soil with its roots so strong that it cannot be uprooted easily. Fierce winds, storms and rain cannot harm grass either. This is the magic of grass!** So, why don't you allow that green magic to engulf you? You are anyway, multi-lingual and you know what you need to do now. Kick start dear, kick start a new life!" he said with a smile.

To cool breeze not only dried her sweat, but also took away her tensions, worries and uncertainties. She imagined herself floating in the air, travelling far, riding on the wind, as it blew over the grassy field.

Raghav, who was playing with the grasses till then, suddenly noticed his mother smiling and was so elated to see his mother smiling that he rushed to his mother and planted a kiss on her cheek.

All these years, Malini had just been surviving; but now she felt that she was ready to life, life for herself. Yes, she was going to stretch herself beyond the horizon, like the green grass. As she hugged Raghav, she grinned, but this time, with nothing to bear at all. She was weightless…

I am He and He is Me!

On whom has the 'Idiot Box' not cast a spell on? While a few belong to the exceptional breed that does not even entertain 'him' as part of their beloved family, I am quite certain that I do not belong to that category. Sunday afternoons is probably the laziest part of the week for everyone and I normally spend the time in front of the idiot box alone, when the rest of the family enjoys a siesta.

But that Sunday afternoon, how I wished my husband was there with me! A channel surfer that I am, flipping between channels was not new that day. For some reason unknown to me I for once held onto one a bit longer. I realized that remote in my hand had remained static for almost two hours. I was immersed in an experience beyond the boundaries that time would define. The movie that I was engrossed so much was **"The Notebook"**. I suggest the married people to watch the movie at least once and I am sure it may eventually become 'as many times as we can'. If I elaborate the content of the movie here, the thrill of watching it may be lost, but to set the context of this article I will have to write a small brief here.

Love at first sight is not something of a fable for a lot of us. So was the case with the two main characters of this masterpiece. The story runs thru the reels of time where the lady suffers from Alzheimer disease in her old age and she forgets everything in the past. The major part of the story revolves around how the husband relives the past, for her and for them, thru a small diary "Notebook". So strong is the bond of love that they remain united in death.

To me the movie was all about the power that love has on humanity and how even in death it prevails. HIS grace created a small space in our hearts for Love, which is even larger than the universe HE created for us. I spent the better part of the afternoon in solitude, my eyes swelled with tears, trying to understand what more HE can give us than this wonderful gift.

In today's context many spend such a lot of time fighting with each other on very trivial things which even lead to divorce. Our culture teaches us that the institution of marriage is far beyond the mundane, a bond that even transcends the physical. The day we are in wedlock we make commitments that are far beyond the murmurings of the mouth in front of a gathered audience or a lit fire. The commitment of my everlasting love to my partner, no matter what challenges I face in life ahead.

A rush of all those beautiful thoughts and "untold" commitments I made in my wedlock, engulfed me. I understood not a bit of anything had changed since then, in spite of all the trivial day to day fights and misunderstanding that we may have had. My prayer from that day on is for The Lord to remind me, each day what a great gift HE has given me and never to forget it even for a moment. I wouldn't ask HIM for more would I? HE has given Love in abundance for not only me but to all.

Ardanareshwara, one of his countless manifestations represents the Shakthi and Shiva as one is it not? *HE exhibits the powerful yet subtle womanhood and the strong yet gentle manhood, sharing equal space and bringing about serenity and harmony in life.*

That wonderful evening helped me to realize the beautiful institution called marriage, far better than what I had so far.

Distinct in physical existence as we are, we need to believe that differences exist and they have to be cherished with the common purpose of celebrating life together. Certain things may never change in our lives. I may never learn to make his favorite meal and he may never learn to even make a tea. I may never attempt to know about his investments and he may never attempt to attend the PTA meets of our children. I may never remember his car number and he may never remember our wedding day. The list goes on and on… ***Yet, at the heart of the hearts we know there would be more and more love between us with each fight and argument. I would be there where he is and he would be there where I would be.***

Certain things are not meant to change - *I am He and He is Me.*

Let's Rise and Shine

I love you, the way you are.
The way you love me, the way I am.

Let us come together for the things we can,
And be at peace when we cannot.

Let our communication not take the one-way highway,
Let's listen as much as we speak.
Let us learn to co-exist, while living lives of our own too.

Let us look to inspire, not influence
And share the power and balance.

Let us not look to bend, but blend,
The way the day blends into the night.

Come Love, Let's Rise and Shine,
Not in toxic Love, but just in Love,
Together and forever.

The More the Merrier

There is very little that he keeps for himself. Retired from the Indian railways around 30 years ago, he has dedicated his life for one purpose. The purpose being to bring about spiritual awareness, in small villages and hamlets in and around the area where he lives. He spent his entire pension benefits towards this cause, donating all his money as and when the opportunity arose. No questions, no references, no doubts whatsoever in his mind, before he makes a donation. He is a busy man even at this ripe age of ninety. He also earns!

Many people throng his home for his sharp astrology skills even from faraway places. He does not charge any fee. He leaves it to the individual to decide what they feel as appropriate. Not a penny from this earning goes to meet his personal needs. Everything is donated to people who seek help from him in spreading spirituality.

Our association with him was by chance some thirty years ago. I have had the privilege of observing him at close quarters right from my young days and each interaction with him had taught me several lessons. My respect for him has grown over the years, not because of his age or his social standing, but because of who he is and what he stands for. The kind of impact that he has created in me and many people around him cannot really be described. His simple but yet powerful persona has changed the way people live their lives. His undeterred trust in the Creator is so profound that anyone who gets associated with him is sure to inherit.

I strongly believe that **Gomathinayagam Thaatha (grandfather)** has never felt the need for money or the support of someone to run his affairs all through his life. All his worldly needs are automatically met. It did sound a bit exaggerated and hyped when people spoke to me about him in the earlier days. But today I see it happening and there is no logic to it. It just happens. If he is in need of some medical assistance, somehow from somewhere that will come. If he thinks of visiting a temple, someone will take him there. His necessities are taken care by someone, somehow or the other. It is very difficult for me to explain how this happens so methodically to him with so much ease. I can only come to a strong conclusion that there is some quality in him that makes these things happen along with his unwavering faith in the Divine. That quality I strongly believe, is closely related to the way he conducts his life. Without doubt that must be one of the main attributes that makes his life run so smoothly. **He has been running his life as "giver" and never a "taker".** Therefore, the more you are a "giver", the more you create space within you to accommodate more and more. When we share something, we somehow connect to others in many ways. In that moment we actually connect with the Creator himself. HE makes things happen, from then on.

I have observed his reaction when someone asks him assistance for a spiritual cause. He never is judgemental and never does question the intent. His "giving" is spontaneous and it flows from within without any blocks. His mind is not occupied by thoughts that either judge it as good or bad. Doubts, questions and benefits occupy tremendous amount of mental space. When the giving is spontaneous and devoid of such thoughts then there is obviously space for more, within. If we hold onto these thoughts we get into a mode of scarcity and the chance to accommodate more from within is reduced. A simple analogy could be that of a paddy field where weeds also grow. If the weeds are removed, I create space to accommodate more paddy saplings. I believe this is exactly what he does.

A lot of us feel constrained. We feel that we do not have enough to give. While that might be true in its literal sense, if we "just think" we can give, then opportunities to give automatically emerge. It might be true that we may be constrained in giving material possessions, but there are many more to give like love, knowledge and the list goes on and on. The space occupied by constraint does not allow anything to get in. Our ability to give more to ourselves therefore reduces too.

Two strangers met in a desolate mountain. One of them did not have a morsel of food as the supplies had run out and was extremely hungry. The other had just enough for one more meal. One stranger who was starving, with much hesitation asked for food to the other. When the other stranger opened the bag to share the food, the hungry stranger saw a precious jewel in the bag. Greed led the stranger to ask for the precious jewel instead of food. The jewel was handed over without any fuss by the other person. The stranger disappeared with the stone only to reappear after some time and he now asked, 'Can you give me something much more precious than this stone? Can you give me that quality within you that made you part with such a precious item with no hesitation what so ever?'

Giving can indeed transform lives. The more we give the more transformed lives we see.

In giving, you give to yourself more, much more than what you give to others. No wonder Gomathinayagam Thaatha is the happiest and most content person I have seen so far in my lifetime. There has never been any expectation in his giving. What will I get out of this, will I benefit from this? These are questions which seemed never to have come to his mind. When one is in such a state then the goodness of life just flows. He is not perturbed by wrong happenings; his health is exceptionally good. He does not pray specifically for anything. I believe that the Grace of the Almighty is always with him, just by the way he conducts his life.

Giving is something much more than Charity. **Would it not be fabulous world, if our prayers everyday were to "get more, to give more" rather than "get more to keep more"?!**

This Moment Matters!

Bubbling with energy like a young puppy, a warm smile with joyful sincerity, as relaxed as a hammock on a pleasant beach, an open mind as that of an infant and so on… I can keep adding many more to this long wish list of delightful qualities that each one yearns to possess. Normally this is also how one would be chosen to be poetic in the description of a young boy or girl in the pink of life. And that is how, I choose to best describe **Seetha,** a close friend of ours, who set her foot into her Senior Citizenship!

I cannot think of any other way of describing her on this day. I may have of course described her very differently some ten years back. I have seen her for over two decades and I should say that I considerably took part in her life journey of crests and troughs in the capacity of a close friend and well-wisher.

'When life gets tough the tough get going,' this timeless proverb mimics her life story in a slightly different viewpoint. Her life progressed smoothly akin to the smooth and graceful autumn rivers till it hit rock bottom. The first catastrophe struck her when she lost her beloved brother to a medical condition that the best of doctors could not cure. She was shaken so badly that it took her quite some time to come out of grief, only to be hit by another. A massive cardiac arrest resulted in the unexpected death of her husband, leaving her alone with her aged parents. The aged couple were solely dependent on her for their livelihood. She accepted what fate had in store for her and decided to move on with a single purpose in mind - to take the best care of her aging parents and provide them the comfort that old age seeks. She was everything to them and so were they. I do not recollect a single day when she left work late, for her parents were eagerly awaiting the arrival of their beloved daughter. She did not compromise on her professional commitments either. At a point in time, her mother could hardly recognize her. She, I presume was gradually taken over by Alzheimer. Feeding, bathing, cleaning and caring were a part and parcel of Seetha's day to day routine activities. She did it with joy and pleasure thanking God every day for the opportunity He had given her to serve her mother. The inevitable then occurred again. Her mother died, leaving her and her father in deep grief. Life had more grief in store for her. It was as bad as it could get. Her father parted very soon after and left Seetha with nothing to look forward in life. Being close to her, I could helplessly see the pain that she was going through. The very little that our family could do was to provide her the solace and courage required to overcome the worst of catastrophes.

The difficult times she underwent seemed to have given her delicate insights into life. She never did make it explicit by words, but her conduct of life thereafter was for everyone to see. I observed her in the next few years slowly moving away from pain to joyfulness and then to bliss. She now had only one thing in mind. Live the moment and live life to its fullest. That frame of mind, set her in a path of exuberance, so distinctly visible to everyone around her. The ordeal that she underwent left an indelible mark on her physical fitness. She could walk only with great difficulty and her footsteps were measured as both her legs had deteriorated significantly. She had an option to give in and stay put within the four walls of the house. But she chose to exercise her "Free Will", to live life to its fullest. A rigorous six month of physiotherapy and unshakable commitment to get back her fitness, saw her get back to her old days and beyond, even to her childhood. I see her today literally bouncing and running around with childish joy and attainment. She has in fact become the brand ambassador for that establishment that helped her physical fitness.

A new-found joy and a blissful path ahead see her indulge in everything with exuberance and joy. She finds joy when she sips a cup of classic south Indian filter coffee. Her eyes sparkle with delight and she makes no attempt to hide it. Her long-lost singing has returned to stay with her. One can overhear her humming the wonderful songs of MS or the tender notes of Pandit Ravi Shankar. I see her reading a lot of books these days with the intensity of a child preparing for examinations. She wants to learn and has even subscribed to an Online certificate course. She finds joy in implementing things she learns then and there. A new recipe that she heard or learnt that day has to be experimented the very day. There is no procrastination. Her hands go up first in a workshop to answer a question - an earnest childlike outburst. She could hire someone for the upkeep of the small but beautiful home she has. She decides against it and finds pleasure in doing things herself. I would not be surprised if she comes to our place driving all by herself or maybe even bi-cycling one day! So much is her persona filled with reverberating energy that I sometimes wonder if she is reborn with a definite purpose that I am just not cognitive off. It seemed to me that God had given her salt when she yearned for water, only to make her understand how prized water is.

Anger fumed inside me several times during those stressful years of hers, as I pleaded with HIM to stop stacking her with agony again and again. Looking back today at her, I comprehend HIS Grace and Mercy. Hardships are enacted only to reveal how beautiful and gentle life can be. When uncomfortable things happen in our life, we blame it all on HIM without realizing that these are for the purpose of making us realize how good the good to come will taste. People who have gone through tough times are blessed in that sense for they emerge more resilient and become inspiration to others. Seetha belongs to that breed for sure. I was possibly ordained to know only later that she was HIS chosen child. Many of us have so much in abundance around us, still we choose to brood on what we don't have instead of feeling grateful about what we have. In the process, we lose out on the present moment. Seetha chose to feel alive even though she had literally nothing to look forward to at a point in time.

I am reminded of the famous book *"A tree grows in Brooklyn" by Betty Smith,* where she goes on to say her prayer, *"Dear God, let me be something every minute of every hour of my life. Let me be gay; let me be sad. Let me be cold; let me be warm. Let me be hungry...have too much to eat. Let me be ragged or well dressed. Let me be sincere - be deceitful. Let me be truthful; let me be a liar. Let me be honourable and let me sin. Only let me be something every blessed minute. And when I sleep, let me dream all the time so that not one little piece of living is ever lost."*

It does look like Seetha digested this book and decided to do just that. Live the Moment and be exuberant about everything. For the past is but a recollect of experiences and the future is nothing but imagination. **This MOMENT is what matters** and make the best of it as it is never ever going to come back. Seetha is an inspiration to many of us. She silently has taught me and to many the *art of living* and particularly the senior citizens, how life can blossom as we age and to live an exuberant life.

Heart to Heart from the Child's Heart!

Hi Friends,

One fine morning, our class teacher asked us, "Should Moral values be cultivated in the children right from their tender age?" This was indeed too big a question for us, a question beyond our comprehension. But wait; is it too big to comprehend?

There is an old saying in Tamil that states that what you learn during infancy is what you carry till your death bed. This is indeed very true and most of us have even seen it happen even at this young age.

I, for example was given so many books by my parents right when I started to recognize pictures. I still remember my mother showing me the huge collection of flash cards every day. My father used to take me to the book store where I browsed each section for hours together. It is beyond any doubt that my fascination for reading was because of this wonderful habit that was cultivated in me right from the age of four. My friends, I am sure that many of you would have such stories to tell. This only goes to prove the old Tamil proverb that I stated at the beginning of this letter.

Therefore, I would tend to believe that Moral values in children will have to be cultivated right from the time we are born. Our parents hold a great responsibility in creating a great environment that will nurture moral values at home. I am told by my elders that during the young age children have the capability to absorb everything more than adults. Children also absorb things whether they are good or bad without bias as they hardly can differentiate between the two. Our first teachers are our parents and we as children absorb whatever they teach us or the way they carry themselves. In our culture Maatha, Pitha, Guru, Deivam in that order are the people who are most important in everybody's life. You will see that our parents stand first in the order. It is therefore important that we learn to respect our parents as the first moral lesson. Most parents think well of their children and would not teach or exhibit bad things. For every parent their child is an asset and they would like to see them as amazing people. While this is true in most cases, it is also quite important that parents take extreme care to conduct themselves, in a way that they become our inspiration for the future.

We spend most of the day time at our school. Our teachers are our parents during the time we are at school. They also wish well for every child in the class without exception. It is therefore equally important that we learn to respect our teachers and absorb as many good things as possible from them. In comparison to parents our teachers play a greater role in creating character and better human beings. I therefore humbly conclude that our teachers are fundamentally the people who create the society and the value systems that it carries. If they fail in their responsibilities, we will all end up in a society that does not carry any moral values. I am reminded of a small poem that I wish to mention here:

There are little eyes upon you and they're watching night and day;
There are little ears that quickly take in every word you say;
There are little hands all eager to do everything you do;
And a little child who's dreaming of the day he will be like you.

Inculcating moral values in children is a hand shake exercise. The first part is the environment we live in. By environment, I mean our parents, our teachers, our school, our lifestyle etc. The second part is we ourselves. Both of these "hands" as I wish to call it should co-exist. Only then a warm hand shake is possible. Even if one of them fails, moral values cannot be nurtured in us. Let me explain this by a small example. If suppose everybody in a particular home wake up late, the child in the home also wakes up late because he or she unconsciously cultivates the habit. Invariably the child is also late to school. Having come late to school, the class teacher is really upset because this has become a habit with the child. The fact that the teacher is upset in the very first period of the day leads the teacher to vent out the anger on the class and in turn the students of the class do not learn much that day because they are diverted. You see, this is what I am referring to as the "environment" and see what a "ripple effect" it can create.

Having talked so long about Moral Values let me explain to you all what it really means. Moral values are essentially a set of principles used to evaluate right versus wrong. It also defines the personal character of a person. Some of the moral values that come to my mind immediately are discipline, honesty, respect for others, kindness, gratitude, responsibility, courtesy etc and the list goes on. For example, if I consider honesty as a moral value, then I would never imagine of telling a lie to my class teacher if I forgot to do my homework. While this is one situation there will be many situations in our lives as we grow up where we may have to be honest. If I am honest in all situations my character gets defined and I get to be recognized as an honest person. Religion plays an important part in building moral values as it builds faith and trust. No wonder our schools give some much importance to spirituality in several ways.

In conclusion, having understood the importance and significance of moral values, can we as children take responsibility in making that "Hand shake" warm, rather than blame everything around us? I am indeed proud that we all have loving parents, fabulous teachers, a wonderful school and a fantastic environment around us. What stops us from practicing more and more moral values? Can we resolve today to pick at least three key moral values that we think is important to each of us and make them a life habit?

I am sure that the world will be a better place with children like us soaked in moral values.

Yours friendly,

Let's Co-Exist?

My husband Ram generally doesn't appreciate or acknowledges my daughters and my crunching and munching pizzas. So, when he finally gave in to the nudging of my daughters, an evening at Pizza Hut, sounded as magical as spending an evening in Paris.

While our Sarathy drove us down, we girls discussed on what we should have on our platter, for the starters, the main course and the yummy dessert. It is a sheer delight to discuss about the cuisines with my girls, as it is the only time, I blissfully ignore to do any permutation combination on calories.

Even before we could take up a seat inside Pizza Hut, Abirami, my first daughter, rang the "Happy Bell" in excitement, making few heads turn towards her with a smile. After placing the order, as we eagerly waited for our delicacies, my second daughter Mathangi, pestered me to take her to the play area in the restaurant.

Since I didn't want the kids to miss out on the experience of fun and food, I took both of them to the play area, which was very spacious, with a cute little cage like thing filled with lot of colorful soft balls. There was only one boy of about eight years, playing inside and his mother standing watching over him.

As both my girls tried to enter the play area, I was little surprised to see the boy being very non-accommodating and refusing to share the space with them. My elder one, Abirami, though just seven years old, got his clear message and stayed away from 'his' space. However, the little one Mathangi, just four, was not ready to compromise. Hence, she went in to the play area and placed herself in a cozy corner to toy around with the balls.

However, she was rudely pushed by the boy who even snatched the balls from her.

Mathangi, out of shock, started to cry aloud and I, feeling powerless in this situation, somehow coaxed her to come out of the play area, but not before I threw a sharp look at the boy's mother. She justified the horrible behavior of her son, by saying, "He just came now, you know! That's why he is being possessive of his space!" Though her justification irked me, I didn't want to pick up an argument. Hence, I brought Mathangi back to our table and tried to distract her by telling her favorite fairy tale.

When the kids began eating the pizza in a sober mood, the pizza guy switched on the Disney channel. Instantly, both the kids forgot the distasteful event and got glued to the television. With a lot of excitement, they watched "The Jungle Book" movie. But I, still a little upset, cribbed to Ram.

Suddenly, my little one Mathangi, pointing at the TV, giggled and in a very excited tone said to her elder sister, "Akka look! The wolf shares its space with the baby!" Momentarily, I stopped grumbling to Ram looked up at the TV. So true, anyone would get enchanted by the beautifully animated scene. The she-wolf with loads of love, affection and twinkling in its eyes, slowly dragged the baby towards its cave welcoming him as the newest addition in the family.

"Ironic, the wolf could accept and accommodate a baby, but here; a kid is not ready to share just a little bit of space with another kid," I thought. Instantly I felt somebody slapping my face as if to say, "Before pointing fingers on somebody, have you been accommodating?"

Honestly, I had not always been accommodating, though the situation demanded it. Once Ram, transferred his air ticket to a woman who desperately wanted to fly down from Pune to Chennai to take care of her father, who had just had a heart attack. I should have appreciated his gesture, yet did I? I only cribbed about the few hours delay in his arrival. Every morning, religiously did I not lecture my children about how to behave – not realizing that they were just little ones who needed to be themselves? And the list goes on…

Many of us, though not deliberately, sometimes are non-accommodating in a situation and we neglect the other side of the story completely. While we fail to co-exist, it causes much trauma, sickness, anger and frustration to the person involved and even to us.

Yes, the little boy had been non-accommodating for his space – yet, wasn't I non-accommodating to his behavior too? After all, he was just a young one who didn't know better. I felt completely rejuvenated as I dropped the brooding and relished every drop of the chocolate sauce spread over the banana fudge. I even dipped my fingers in the sauce and licked it, along with my girls. I grinned at Ram, when he gave me a quizzical look, wondering how the mood climate had changed so swiftly.

Once we were outside, I gazed up. ***The trillions of stars, the moon, a few tufts of white clouds all seemed to co-exist so peacefully in the skies. None fought for space, and yet each had 'enough'.*** I realized then, that everything in nature exists in perfect harmony because they all accommodate each other. What the other did or did not do was none of my business, but I decided that I would surely become much more accommodating in life. Co-existing was a possibility. In fact, co-existing was the answer. **Let's co-exist?**

Did you visit yourself?

"Oh no!" a scream pierced the air, as Arjun entered home. It was his wife, Ananya, who screamed at the top of her voice. Ananya shouts but she never screams. This gave him jitters. He didn't have the patience to climb the steps, so he skipped and jumped over the steps, rushed to the room only to find Ananya screaming at the kids.

Unable to control his anger, Arjun shouted at Ananya, "Just because you happen to be the mother, you can't scream at the kids. I am just fed up, completely fed up with you!" Ananya, looked incredulous, completely shaken, dumbfounded, just let her tears speak. But unfortunately, that day, Arjun was in no mood to hear her tears. What happened to the otherwise kind, soft natured Arjun that day?

Ananya and Arjun led a happy life with two little cute kids, amidst fights, arguments, laughs, smiles, giggles, agreements and disagreements, bonded in true love. Never once had anyone found Arjun raising his voice or losing his temper. Even if hell broke loose, he would never lose his cool, but would find a good way to come out of it. His soft smile was a magnet for love.

The destiny decided to smile upon Arjun, that he started experiencing extreme pressures at professional front. More he tried to put up a brave face, more bouts came his way. Night and day he was engulfed by targets, timelines, assessments and appraisals that the job dis-satisfaction was breaking him. He came to a stage where he couldn't take it further. To add woes to his already mounting problems, his wife Ananya was complaining of acute back pain that he couldn't tolerate watching her suffer.

On that day, Ananya took some pain killers, thanks to the pills, feeling dizzy she dozed off. When she woke up it was almost close to six in the evening and all her chores including making her kids do their school work had gone for a toss. Though fatigued, yet she somehow managed to have both the kids beside her, to help them finish their work. Kids as they are, they worked, they played and that led to fight and both of them were at loggerheads! Extremely exhausted Ananya gave out a cry.

Arjun, after a strenuous day at work, entered home and the scream from inside left him in jitters!

After his words shot Ananya like arrows straight from the quiver, Arjun too felt the pain. But he was too drained to reciprocate to Ananya's tears; instead, he turned back to his car to take a drive.

As he drove, the gentle breeze caressed his face. He introspected. He realised, he had become little weaker, less tolerant and a little frustrated too. He wasn't himself. It was then he asked himself, **"When was the last time I visited myself?"** "Not in the recent past!" came the answer.

Arjun, knew the answer for all his problems lies within self. He needs to make a new beginning to discover himself. Yes, his visit to himself is long due and it cannot wait anymore!

Next day, at the crack of dawn, leaving behind his i-pad, i-phone, and the buzzling Chennai, just with a thin baggage, Arjun drove down to lay his head on the lap of his home town, to the land of enchanting natural beauty, Coonoor, to be with himself.

Reaching Coonoor, Arjun sat on one of the rocks on the soft rounded upland, watching the clumps of mountain forests, nestled amongst undulating grassy hills. He was ecstatic about the God's exquisite work of tapestry being woven with meticulous care.

He helplessly fell in the spell of the beguiling beauty that his excitement too was uplifted with the crisp clean air. Being there amidst nature, with nothing to do, except to be with himself, sort of became his meditation. Sitting beside the river bank, he enjoyed the **incredible visual images of calmness and tranquillity of the quiet river.** He heard himself – he listened.

As he experienced the tranquillity, he allowed the stillness envelop every cell of him. His mind and body relaxed like never before. **As he relaxed, he felt the release of tension and his return to equilibrium.** How true! The time spent to oneself, helps them to mentally, physically, spiritually, socially, realise themselves!

In that state, he felt some clarity in his thought process. The disheartening situations revealed some heartening truths. He was ready to take some exciting and enduring decisions. It dawned to him, that he was finally happy to embrace the better life that was born out of his dissatisfaction.

That instant he pictured Ananya's teary face, startled by his insensitive behaviour, in his mind. Feeling the urgent need to pacify her, he immediately messaged her, "Serene Places change people's mind and heart for good! I realise myself."

In a jiffy, his soft smile decorated his face, yet again, as he read the reply, "I know..! Serene Places change good people's mind and heart even better!"

Life - A Fairy Tale

A quiet spring day graced by the cool breeze

Perfect ambience to mate pen and paper

Lured by the setting I succumbed to a dream

A dream that would take me back in time

As far as my memory could project

A quiet assessment of life thus far in solitude

Exposed a beautiful secret

A fairy tale brimming with goodness

A tale called Life, unfurled to its fullest

Putting up a brave face, the bravest ever

Standing on the small bench

Reprimanded by a caring teacher

For being loquacious in kindergarten class

The gloomy little face posing for a group photo

Compelled to partake in the customary annual event

The hide and seek with the aged grandmother

Unrelenting in the game of search

Sense of achievement at the top of the guava tree

Plucking the luscious ripe fruit

Waves of tender reflections…..

A fairy tale brimming with goodness

A tale called Life, unfurled to its fullest

The good, bad and ugly, events in the life

All filled with emotions unexplained

One by one as they unfurled with ease

From innocent infancy to vibrant adolescence

From school to college and then to work

Each one expressing itself with utmost charm

All the same nevertheless, reliving the past in the present

Had the greatest of lessons to be imparted

One too many to recollect each and every one

Life bloomed to be the greatest of Gurus

A fairy tale brimming with goodness

A tale called Life, unfurled to its fullest

Why wait for the forties, fifties, sixties or beyond?

To sit at ease and review the past

Now is the time, this is the moment, everyday

Life is ready to impart if I wish to receive

I despise myself for walking the memory lane so late

No qualms though having been given quite a plate full now

To last the rest of my life,

I recon reviews happen here and now

Not in the future at an unknown destination

This quiet spring day eased me into a world of charm

Results I know not yet, but sure I am

Ready to learn from the Guru called Life

For life is a gift not to be wasted

It's a fairy tale, brimming with goodness

A tale called Life, unfurled to its fullest.

Believe Him as He believes in You!

My office was abuzz with activities, as we were organising a congregation for all our customers. After a plenty of discussions, meetings, chalk and talk, about budgeting, selecting and reserving the site, acquiring permits, and coordinating transportation and parking etc., my staff were both anxious and excited, about the event which was scheduled to happen the subsequent weekend.

We chose a massive open ground with a huge space earmarked for parking, as we were expecting a few hundreds of our customers and other stakeholders of our company, to attend.

While the D-day was nearing, I shook in shock, as the weather predictions grimed at me with an unseasoned rainfall being expected that week.

With everything set, what will I do now? This event being so close to my heart, a project organised by our company as a fund-raising campaign for the upliftment of destitute women and parentless kids, how would I ever call off the event? As I thought and thought, nothing came to my mind to tackle the situation.

With heart and mind laden with sorrow, eyes welled-up with tears; I raised both my hands to the Almighty, profusely praying to help me in the time of distress.

Having left everything to HIM, somehow, I slowly started to believe that everything would go on smoothly. Yet, in the corner of my mind, I kept questioning myself. Am I doing the right thing to go by my belief? Would I be regretting for my wrong decision by going ahead with the event?

With strong winds getting intensified as stormy winds, that night it started raining cats and dogs, and heavy clouds covered my mind. Tears dropped from my eyes, as the heavens 'tears' dropped on the ground! The drip and the drop, made my heart beat drop!

How could this be happening, when the day after was supposed to be the big day for me? How could my Lord turn deaf ears to my cries?

With no time to think and no choice to make, crestfallen, I scheduled for an urgent meeting for the next day, to give my staff instructions regarding cancellation of the event and about information that are to be sent across to all stakeholders.

Completely drenched and drained, I reached home and went to bed with a heavy heart. After few hours of tossing in the bed, I dwelled into deep sleep.

Next morning, I woke up with a jolt, as the sun rays pierced my skin through the window pane.

Throwing away the bed sheet, I rushed to the balcony, with every cell of mine occupied by guilt. Tears rolled unguarded as I watched the beautiful Sun winking at me, as if to say "Go ahead Kiddo! Gear up for your work!"

What can I say about the kindness of my Lord? How could I ever attempt to describe HIS love? HE accepted my prayers and HE changed the course of the day, for me!

But I? I failed to believe in HIM. I failed to trust HIM. I failed to understand the power of surrender! I failed to comprehend the term 'Leaving unto thee.'

That moment, my heart was opened. I learnt a lesson from life. **"Putting God first, yielding to God's Presence in our lives, unveils a surprising fact: We don't always have to make things happen; they can happen by themselves. Neither must we always have a plan or be in control."**

It would be impertinent to describe or boast how happy we were and how many smiles were lit up because of the stupendous success of the event. Was it all our work? Thank You Lord, for teaching me to believe YOU as YOU believed in me.

Never Alone!

I entered with my aunt, to attend the Radha-Krishna Kalyanam at a devotee's house. The hall was dazzling with beautifully decorated Diyas. There were over fifty ladies singing the bhajans loudly, and yet I kept finding myself drawn to a simple woman sitting cross legged, wearing a white sari. There was a grace about her that made it appear like she wasn't singing the prayer, but feeling it.

As the Radha-Krishna dandiya dance began, I was once again amazed by that lady, who danced joyfully and swirled her dandiya with such energy, that, the 20s in the room stood no match to this woman obviously in her 70s!!!

Little later, I sat by her, to get to know her better. After my self-introduction, she introduced herself as Kausalya amma, who with her radiant smile, shone much brighter than the diyas lit around the hall. What an angelic smile, it was! Somehow, I felt in the crowded hall, she and me were all alone. She told me that she lived nearby and added, that she lived all alone. There was no sadness or self-pity attached to her words – just mere facts spoken with strength and acceptance. As she spoke about her bhajan classes for children, her love for discourses and discos, Ramacharitramanas and Rajinikanth, I fell in love with this bundle of energy and asked her if I could come and meet her once in a meanwhile. Her response was a warm hug and the words, "Of course, my dear."

Since then, my day never ended without a tea break with Kausalya amma, who welcomed me with that characteristic smile and warm hug. Every single day was an experience in itself, for both mind and body, as she showcased her culinary skills along with her knowledge and wisdom. As I chewed and relished the delicacies, the mind always had enough food for thought with the discussions, arguments, dis-agreements and agreements between us.

One day, one of Kausalya amma's neighbours brought her newly born grand-daughter, to seek her blessings. I already knew Kausalya amma was a magnet, a magnet of love and divinity and yet the fact that her neighbour placed her one among sages, asking for her blessings on the birth of the child, surprised me. After the neighbour left, as if she read my mind, "Gayathri" she called out and said, "These people around, think that I am a picture of love, embodiment of Meera and some kind of sage, without a spotless character. They just won't and don't want to understand my bitter past."

As if in deep thought, with eyes closed, she continued, "I am that child, who lost her mother at three, abandoned by father at six, grew up at the mercy of my aunt, till sixteen. Never knew what love, kind, gentle, caring, soothing words were. Not a single day passed by, without shedding tears in front of the lord, for the pathetic life he had thrown at me. I joined my first job at nineteen in an organization, reeking with jealousy and ruthless aggression. I, just twelfth standard graduate, learnt the nuances of accounting procedures, and quickly started shining through in the company, due to my urgent need to prove to myself and the world that I was worth it," she paused and sipped her tea.

Then she continued, in a matter-of-fact voice, "I made some money but was still longing for that love and care! It was then, during one of the conferences that my company chairman met me. That multi-millionaire fell in love with this dynamic young woman. As a person who was clueless and nobody to give directions, I instantly trusted him with my life. He shifted my residence to his newly constructed bungalow; we led a life of husband and wife, though there wasn't any formal announcement. My happiness didn't last long. The first big blow came, when I conceived. He pleaded to abort it and promised he would marry me, if I did so. As a person, who had no life apart from him, I bowed to his wish, not knowing the fact that this drama is going to repeat a few more times. You don't know that I conceived and aborted six kids, did you, Gayathri?" She smiled. I could see that she had been healed of the past pain. There was no trace of bitterness in her words. I sat enthralled, unable to say a single word, waiting to hear her.

Moments later, she continued, "I believed that things were never going to look up. I felt completely devastated. With heavy heart and tears streaming down from the eyes, I bowed before the lord, to seek an answer to my question, which was lingering in my mind for years. WHY ME FOR ALL TROUBLES MY LORD, WHY ME ALONE? Not able to contain myself, I looked up deep into Krishna's eyes, for an answer. That instant, that moment, I was made to realize that all along I had thought it was "I", who was alone in this tragic life. "I" was looking for that love, care and guidance. "I" who had to struggle through. Yet, was I alone? Could I ever be alone? It seemed as if Krishna himself was laughing and answering, "I am always with you. Always. I will be that guiding force, that Parthasarathy, forever. Give your life in my hands."

As that beautiful realization dawned, everything about my being changed. That elusive love had been found. I quietly moved out of the chairman's palatial bungalow, to follow the footsteps of my Divine Friend. Based on my previous job-experience, I started afresh in a new company – a much gentler, humbler and compassionate me. Through grit and determination, I climbed the corporate ladder and also managed to complete my post-graduation along the way. What followed after those were the new environment, new job, accolades, appreciations, promotions and above all Satsang!" said she.

Little later, as she finished her tea, with a soft smile, in a completely energized tone, said, ***"When I gave up everything and surrendered to HIM, my Krishna became everything for me. He became the loving mother, whom I had never known. He became that beloved father, I never had. He became that beloved husband that I always desired. He became those beloved kids that I could never experience. Since then, when troubles hit me, I never feel wobbly because I know He is with me! People around me see me for what I am and love me, but He loved me even when I didn't know what the meaning of the word is. What better life could I have asked for…?"*** She had tears of love and gratitude in her eyes.

I was feeling choked with emotions, however, Kausalya amma, completely unperturbed, got up and went to her room. Wiping my tears, I smiled as I watched her, light a diya before her Lord. She had left me with a strength that I had never known before. Even with a life full of riches, love and family, I felt so alone at times, and here she was, an embodiment of strength and faith, ***alone and yet never alone.***

Am I There?

The child beheld the majestic mountains,

Soaking in its air of mystique beauty,

She closes her eyes, and envisions what lies beyond,

The unknown behind the known form.

"Have I reached?", she asks into the silence,

Waiting for His answer, to offer her guidance.

Smiling, He echoes her question back to her,

"I don't know, are you here yet?"

"No, Lord. I fear I am not,

For there is still a **You** *shaped hole in my heart"*

"Then have you tried walking the path to calm yourself?" he asks.

"Not very well, for it has taken me to task."

"With neither peace nor calm to fill your mind, where do you put your roots?"

"Grounded, I am not my lord, for this path is yet to give me fruits."

"Will you look beyond yourself; will you still reach?"

"Indeed, I shall. Not by being a doormat for everyone, but a doorstep for each."

"With what you have gained now, will you be here?"

"With Calm and Peace, Compassion and Wisdom, I shall be there, My Lord""I shall be!"

Life and Beyond

"Charu, please, why don't you drive?" asked Chandru. "No way, I am enjoying every moment of this drive being on the passenger's seat and you want me to leave this comfort and get into driving mode? No way! No How!" winked and giggled Charu. "Oh, come on Charu, don't talk rubbish. I am extremely tired and I am not going to drive further. Please dear, you drive now," pleaded Chandru. Charu smiled and took over the wheels in her hand, allowing Chandru the much-deserved break. She was confident about her driving... and yet... Oh, oh, OOOOOOOOH!

As Charu opened the broken car door and got down, she was mystified! "Where am I and what is this place?" thought she, completely confused and perplexed.

As she walked a little further, she understood, she was magically transformed to a wonderland. The atmosphere was so new, something that no being could have explored and so breathtaking. Even the greatest of poets would be stuck for words because how one could even attempt to describe such magnificence. Can she call it just plains? Yes and No. Yes, there was nothing at all. Yet, No. Because she was powerless to believe that there is nothing at all. The beauty, the radiance around, enveloped every cell of hers. Did she see the splendor of seas, painted rainbow in the sky? Did she smell the freshness of spring? No. Yet, she experienced everything of those. She was scintillated as she felt the gentle breeze caressing her. And how would ... could she describe further? It was simply miraculous, beyond this; she didn't know how to explain herself.

Was this 'the place', she had feared all her life? Was this Death? Was this what she had been so scared, horrified and terrified about?   There was no thorny path, no darkness and nothing eerie at all about this place.

Yes, she was all-alone and, in that loneliness, for the first time she felt ecstatic, elated, exuberant and energetic. What could she possibly miss here? She knew that she was in 'THE' place, 'the ultimate destination' - the summit of peace, harmony, tranquility, silence and serenity - the dwelling place of the Supreme.

She was in a state of trance as she experienced the happiness, joy, warmth - 'the bliss'.

It was then she heard this whisper, "My child, you will come back here, but a little later. Now, let's go back!" "But Lord, why not here, now?" she thought. Instantly she heard the whisper again, "This beautiful experience is just to show you that there is no reason for you to fear death. With this endured gift, you would enjoy and treasure every moment of your beautiful life too. You will come back dear, but now we must leave."

 Even before she could object, she was moving backwards.

She suddenly heard some voices. "I am sorry, Mr. Chandru. In spite of all my efforts, I couldn't save your wife!" announced the doctor.

"How could this be Doc; how could this be? It can't be doc!" cried Chandru.   "She just took a drastic left turn to avoid any collision against the lorry. While doing so, she banged her head on the steering and lost her conscious. There was no bleeding or any visible external injury and now you say it is all over? No doc No! Please do something about it. She could have just got into a state of shock. Her heart could have just skipped a beat or two but it would not have stopped. Please doc. Please!" whimpered Chandru, with folded hands and knees down, and with tears streaming down from his eyes.

Suddenly Charu gulped for air and started coughing. The doctor rushed out of ICU and screamed "Mr.Chandru! Miraculous. She is back!" in excitement.

Chandru, unable to contain his excitement, rushed into the ICU, to see his Charu, alive.

As Charu slowly opened her eyes, she witnessed Chandru smiling with tears trickling down from his eyes. She too smiled back. *Chandru smiled because his prayers had been answered. The much wiser, and yet humbler, Charu smiled back, because of her discovery that life beyond life too was beautiful... and there was nothing to actually be afraid of. Somehow everything around seemed more colourful, more beautiful and more accentuated to Charu.* She watched Chandru who was kissing her hands and repeating the words, "You're alive, you're alive..." and said, in a voice weak in volume, but strong in determination, **"Yes I'm alive. So alive..."**

Higher .. Deeper .. And Beyond !!

A vacation! The very thought is thrilling! A vacation as a mother! The very thought is exciting! A vacation just as wife! The very thought is…………..!

That is how I felt…. speechless, when Ram my husband said that we both would be on a week-long vacation to the land of GNH - Bhutan – the lonely planet, which fiercely guards its traditions.
The very next week, I was holding on to my beloved in the aircraft that zigzagged the deep-cut valleys without smashing into the terraced slopes, exposing us to the mystical and spiritual land.

The first few days, we were taken through the land of stunning natural scenery, shown around the trove of archaeological treasures, ornate temples and splendid dzongs. The afternoon before our last day stay at Bhutan, our young, every smiling travel guide, showed me the picture of a place of our next day visit, known as 'Tiger's Nest'

The picture was worth a thousand words … the colours, the clouds, the outcrops and the temperature combined created an eerie but an enchanting vista. However, it was not a destination I wanted to be even in my wild dreams. I am this girl, brought up completely in plains, with absolutely no knowledge of hilly terrain or trekking.

And I have to confess, I have altitude sickness. The very thought of height, can bring the worst out of me.

But Ram being a go-getter, gave an enchanting smile and said, "Trust me. I am there with you!"

That evening, I once again vehemently opposed the travel to the cliff situated over 10000 feet high and opted to stay out of the trip. But he calmed me, assured me that he had made arrangement for a mule to carry me uphill. I heaved a sigh; not knowing what was in store for me the next day and hit the bed.

That bright morning, I stood at the foot of the cliff. One look at the mule, I knew I had signed in for the most dangerous travel option. The wind was chilly and I was grumpy.

After the basic instructions on horse ride, I was made to sit on the mule. I didn't have much time to complain. The mule started to carry me from the valley, through the trail slowly and gently, climbed into a pine forest where we passed by several structures containing water-powered prayer wheels surrounded by prayer flags. It was gratifying to look at Ram, as he rode on the mule like a pro. Though the same could not be said about me.

Some minutes of upward travel, I knew I had signed my death warrant. What started off as a simple trail slowly transformed into a steep, arduous, steady climb up to the ridge. The mule veered on the edge, scaring me to the death. Just one misstep could cause a huge fall. My depth of respiration increased and I heard my inner voice cautioning, "Don't look down. Don't die on the mountains!"

There was nothing I could do to obliterate the fear factor. There was no tag of grown up, independent woman, mother and wife within me anymore. I cried like a baby. Wailing, howling, weeping and pleading to drop me off from the mule. Ram and the guide were not prepared for this experience. With face turning red in embarrassment, Ram let me down from the mule. But just for that moment.

This time I was adamant and determined to hike, giving the mule the much-deserved freedom. Some steps forward, I knew hike was not going to be easy either. The path became steeper, the air thin, dry and crisp. Hiking at high elevation had me pulling in oxygen with audible gasps.

Looking at me huffing and puffing, Ram and the guide were not ready to take any risk. Apparently, I was not going to make it even 50 m further. Ram chose to stop the journey and return back. Nevertheless, I knew at the heart of hearts how much he was excited about this trip and I appealed to him to move forward. Would he leave me in the middle of nowhere or send me back to the valley alone? Both Ram and Guide again persuaded me to take the mule. Being caught in a catch-22 situation, I once again ascended on the mule, this time with eyes shut and lips engaged in prayers. The guide became my 'Real Guide' as he walked beside me throughout the uphill journey.

Finally, after an hour of seemingly eternal climb, we stopped for this magnificent view of the monastery. The vista of the monastery and the valley was beyond spectacular. It was absolutely worth the climb.

It looked like we could touch the monastery from the viewpoint. But it was a wishful thinking; it was still on the far end of the deep valley. From here, the trail turned into steep descending steps before it climbed up again, over 700 steps in all.

Completely exhausted and flabbergasted I asked myself, "Why did I sign up for this deathly trip!" My body ached from the climb—my feet, ankles, calves and knees, my throat and my head. But could I expose myself and let Ram regret? I said to myself "I am OK. I made it this far. Just few more…" However, the steps were even steeper and my legs trembled in fear. I forgot about the humiliation and traveled the distance down to the waterfall on my bum.

As I climbed up again from the waterfall to reach the monastery, I couldn't battle with anxiety anymore. Ram was some steps forward. The fear of fainting engulfed me. My eyes darkened and I felt as though my end was nearing. Crazy thoughts and images of my kids and parents wrapped my mind. That moment, tears trickled from my eyes. I fervently prayed to the Divine Mother to come to my rescue.

How would The Divine Mother not hear the plea of her child? Even if it is 10000 feet above, in the middle of nowhere, would that matter to the All-pervasive force?

That very moment, I faintly heard a voice calling, "Dear lady, you don't look good. Please sit on the rock." I turned and saw a short Chinese lady, smiling at me. She held my hand and assisted me to the nearby rock. Ram too by then looked back and rushed towards me.

She noticed my palms had turned dark. She massaged at some pressure points, helped me breathe. After ten long minutes of her motherly care, I felt completely energized. Ram and I were lost for words to express our gratitude. When enquired about her profession, she mentioned that she is an acupuncture therapist from China. She hugged me and bade good bye, while I wondered how would I even attempt to decipher the mystery behind the Chinese lady appearing from nowhere to help me during the time of dire need? It was something Higher, Deeper and Beyond my little knowledge and thinking ability. It was very evident that we were made to experience the Power of Unknown.

It was exhilarating to finally reach Tiger's Nest Monastery. The atmosphere throughout the monastery was mystical. We were enveloped with a deep sense of calmness and peace. With tears flowing from my eyes, I knelt on the rough wooden floor before the Deity and offered my prayers in silence.

It is told that The Guru Rinpoche the Deity of the temple went through eight different incarnations on that very spot. *In a way I felt that He helped me incarnate into a better person. The day that started as a tourist ended as a pilgrim. The day that started with wailing ended with peace. The day that started with skeptic thoughts transformed into a feel of incredibly invincible at the end.*

Descending the long path, I could see everything clearly, with a feeling of lightness.

The Divine Invitation

It must be around a decade since I set my sight on a photo that got etched in my memory for ever. The photo was on my desk all the while and was inadvertently the first darshan everyday morning. Myself and my hubby felt extremely attracted to the place initially and wanted to be there somehow, someday.

Attraction gradually turned to yearning and were ever present in the back drop of our mind like the gentle breeze over the calm seas. The past few months were a combination of excitement and anxiety, as we awaited medical clearance, after a battery of fitness tests. At last, it was happening!

Just to think that we were closer to our dream destination, **Mt. Kailash,** was itself so engrossing that we could hardly let our minds wander into other things. Everything else seemed to be too trivial to even warrant observation. All these years, we were certain of one thing though. If we were bestowed the opportunity of being in Kailash, we would not be there as a tourist, neither a thrill seeker, nor a nature lover, not even as a pilgrim. Even if it is for just a moment, we wanted to be there as a seeker, for sure. When that turned reality, we could not thank HIM enough for His Invitation. All that we could do was to shed tears of joy and gratitude, every day, for we were not capable of anything more than that.

What more can you ask for when you are accompanied by a group of likeminded people? The long road journey of seven days to the foothills turned out to be the one that was soaked in longing and devotion. The instant we started our Parikrama

(Circumambulation of the sacred hill) from the foothills, all apprehensions of our physical ability to undergo the trek became a part of the past! Some unknown but ubiquitous force seemed to lead us with every footstep that we even did not feel our feet touch the ground. The panting for breath, a common symptom at altitudes of 17, 000 feet showed no signs of occurrence or we were simply oblivious to it. Just the magnificence and splendour of one of the most sacred places on Earth was consuming every part of our body. Even the elderly who had opted for assistance for the Parikrama in the earlier part of the journey saw no need for it anymore. Why would someone need assistance when HE was there besides us always! In fact, they turned out to be inspiration for the younger folks! Be it the snow-clad scintillating view in the calm twilight, or the dazzling gold cover in the spirited dawn, or the sheer grandeur of the structural formation resembling scriptural characters etched in the mountain slants, all emphasised one significant thing. HIS omnipresence everywhere! Involuntarily we were but uttering HIS name and glory with earnestness and devotion as never before.

Basking in the grace of the most sacred mountain, meditation was but so natural. The vast terrain studded with several mountains, each of a different making, the steady flow of the river from Kailash peaks on either side, the gentle but cold winds caressing our faces, a comfortable warm day time and still night times with the bright moonlight spreading her grace…it was nothing but ecstasy all the time. Two full days in HIS presence was a great boon for us. Elaborating further would only be a play of words and will in no way reflect the individual experiences that each of us prized.

Being to oneself literally in such a powerful energy space naturally led me to contemplation. For me, contemplation has always been a great tool that aids inner transformation. It threw open to me several life lessons in the backdrop of this sacred place. The most significant one was on how a pilgrimage can transform someone. The energy and the physical alertness that was dominant at the beginning of the long journey, slowly started to dwindle as we progressed towards our destination each day. The willingness to reach the destination, though, never ever faded. Physical, mental, climatic and logistic challenges became part and parcel of our being during this time. We gradually gave in to all of them and accepted that moment, just as it was. Without us realizing it then, a silent inner revolution was constantly taking place. **We were slowly loosening up on our identity!** It really did not matter to which caste or community I belonged to or if I were a CEO or a peon or even a male or female. The resistance from within gradually started to hit rock bottom. One might argue that this was possibly because of the tiring travel at high altitudes. So be it, but the outcome nevertheless was so significant. That's all mattered to me. In fact, in the last part of the yatra I had not even seen my own face for four full days! **Therefore, when I set foot on Kailash, it was a love affair between HIM and me. Nobody and nothing separating us!** It was then that I understood the meaning as to why such sacred places are always available, yet at difficult grasp. It is just to get you down on your knees, humbled with no resistance what so ever. **That is the only way when I can become receptive to HIS Grace!** Wouldn't that be the longing intent of any pilgrimage? I would have progressed if I had achieved that much at least. I found meaning in what the great saint Manikavasagar said in the famous Tamil spiritual hymn Thiruvasagam. "I as a mortal did nothing. I just kept myself open with no resistance, and you poured yourself into me. I am not the smart one. YOU are the one. Can I ever repay you Oh benevolent one?"

Yes, I thought. I will not be able to repay, but can I do something that will reduce me a little more and get me closer to YOU? What better way to it than to leave behind something of me and get a little more of HIM into me. My dear friend *(my ego)*, was nudging me constantly by way of repetitive reminders of accomplishment all along the descend. "I made it, I am privileged, only a gifted few have made it here!". The Divine showed me the correct path again in the form of a Tibetan pilgrim. The pilgrim was completely engrossed with one of the most physically challenging activity, making her way slowly up towards Kailash. She was starting her parikrama literally on all four, by performing body-length prostrations. She bent down, knelt, did full length prostration, rose to her knees, prayed and then crawled forward on hands and knees to start the next prostration. I pinched myself to reality, as I saw the pilgrim progressing the Parikrama on all fours. I found myself sobbing like a baby, in awe and admiration of her devotion and surrender to the Divine. My legs gave in and I found myself prostrating at her feet. With all the support systems in place, here I was claiming pride to an achievement and in contrast the pilgrim who bothered not about anything, not even someone falling at her feet. I felt **reduced** to a size of insignificance. I spent the next hour in solitude. Can I earnestly give up my mental makeup to become humbled again and a million times more? Yes, it is more difficult than giving away a fruit or vegetable of like or dislike after a pilgrimage! But the try is worth it, I decided. My prayers thereafter to the Lord have been to provided me the opportunities to be humbled again and again.

Pilgrimage has always been an intrinsic part of our culture from days yore and with purpose. History tells us that pilgrimages to the remote and sacred destinations have always transformed people and many have become the Great Gurus and Masters that we know of today. I know for sure that I have tried earnestly to leave behind some of my baggage. I do not yet know what I took back from the pilgrimage. Maybe someday I will get to realize it through another pilgrim like the Tibetan. But for now, the only thing that I can feel and live-in gratitude, is HIS invitation to experience a little bit of HIM.

"Nayir Kidayai Kidantha Adiyerkku,Thayir Chirantha
Dhayavana Thatthuvane"

"Kadayavanenai Karunaiyinaal Kalandhu Aandu Konda
Vidayavaney"

"You have but taken mercy on this lowly one and showed much more mercy than even a mother, to me who was lying even worse than the last of the dogs." (Tamil Spiritual Scripture: *Tiruvasagam*)

Oh Lord grant me the chance of once again being with you in your abode.

He and Me

Zenith in lavish foliage,
Held together by imposing rocks
Tender clouds cuddling the contours
Yearning gaze through my window
The mountain in the distance
In the on-setting twilight
Was but a beautiful dream!
How delightful it would be
To set foot on this glorious creation
Emotions and expressions were but profound
The very sight, though far in the distance
I longed to be there one day
Invited sooner than I hoped for

Childish excitement knew no boundaries

Energy and aggression at peak

I ascended the shrubbery to the top

Distinctly different to what I saw

My window gaze seemed so untrue!

I saw no rock anymore

The majestic structures turned real

Naturally sculpted to perfection

They were but the finest from the Sculptor

Grace and elegance brimming with Life

As my observation grew intense

Rocks disappeared into oblivion

Profound in full blossom,

Life and Life is all I could see!

I saw no clouds anymore

As the moisture touched my face

Drifting gently like a stream

They were no longer water forms

Or fairies swaying around

As my observation grew intense

Clouds and mist just gone

Profound in full blossom,

Life and life is all I could see!

I saw no greenery anymore

My feet hesitated to set foot

Fearful of destroying the delicate

Wonderful assortment of vegetation

Dancing in harmony to the gentle breeze

As my observation grew intense

Non-existent were the trees and bushes

All were like chatty neighbours

Conversing a language of their own

Inviting me to their dwelling

Profound in full blossom,

Life and life is all I could see!

Soaked in gratitude and solitude

Time passed in a jiffy

Left with no option to choose

The descend was but unwilling

I graciously let myself down

Knowing more of HIM now

Feeling life in the animate and inanimate

Delicate, gentle yet reflective

Senses knew no bound

Ecstasy to the core

Unveiled to me by the Creator

Profound in full blossom,

Life and life is all I could see!

Opportunity! Will it knock again?

For the ascend to arise again

I cry, pray in ecstasy,

Bestow these moments all the time

Here or there, far or near

Mountains or valleys, deserts or seas

For me and everyone around me

I promise to thee,

I will strive to be intense

To behold YOU within and around me

Profound in full blossom,

Life and life is what I see!

www.ingramcontent.com/pod-product-compliance
Lightning Source LLC
LaVergne TN
LVHW041152180726
843490LV00005B/1677